Meister Eckhart

Ursula Fleming was born into a Catholic family in Liverpool in 1930, her mother being a doctor and her father a surgeon. At the age of six she was diagnosed as a musician and won her first festival two years later. At fifteen she gave up Catholicism and her musical training, turning instead to the study of relaxation, a subject she has taught for many years, latterly as a means of pain control in major surgery.

She first read Eckhart in her early twenties, and has since talked about him in convents, monasteries and religious houses throughout the British Isles. In 1980 she started a petition for his rehabilitation in the Catholic Church. She had earlier regained her faith and is now a lay Dominican.

Ursula Fleming worked for some time at both a hospice and a Pain Relief Unit, and now works at one of the major London hospitals and in Harley Street.

Meister Eckhart:
The man from whom
God nothing hid

Edited by:
Ursula Fleming

Templegate Publishers
Springfield, Illinois

First published in Great Britain by
Fount Paperbacks, London in 1988

Copyright in this collection © Ursula Fleming

First Published in the United States in 1990 by
Templegate Publishers
302 East Adams
P.O. Box 5152
Springfield, Illinois
62705

ISBN 0-87243-176-2

Library of Congress Catalog Number 89-51798

Contents

Introduction

In compiling this book I have used the translation of C. de B. Evans dated 1924 Book 1 and 1931 Book 2.

This may rouse the ire of some academics, I know. There has been much work done recently in authenticating texts, and there have been new and more accurate translations from the German, notably that of M. O'C. Walshe published by Watkins 1979.

If I had had the option I might well have bowed to opinion and used other, more modern translations, but I did not have that option, and in going back to C. de B. Evans and the books I have known and lived with for over thirty years I was much more at home.

I have no knowledge of who C. de B. Evans was, or is, but I have no doubt that she was a remarkable woman and I am deeply indebted to her firstly for recognizing the quality of Meister Eckhart at a time when he was virtually unknown, and then for making his works available in English. Translating the work of a man of Meister Eckhart's calibre is not a job for the mediocre, the faint-hearted or the uninspired.

Her use of words is concise but also at times poetic, and this is why I have avoided modernizing the text. I have avoided quoting from the pieces which M. O'C. Walshe states are not truly by Eckhart. But this book is not meant for scholastics. They would have no need for it. Nor is it meant for the hippy fringe in the States who have adopted Eckhart as some sort of mystic guru. It is meant for the sort of people to whom I have talked about Eckhart for the past thirty years, ordinary, intelligent people whose wish is to strengthen their knowledge of the Christian faith and to discover the truth, like those who came on the courses I gave, usually at Spode House which, until its closure in July 1987, was the Dominican Conference Centre in Staffordshire.

The choice of extracts has been made with the aim of clarifying and categorizing some of Eckhart's teaching, so that those who, like myself, have had no specific theological training may find his works more accessible and will no longer find the books of his "Sermons and Collations" daunting.

*

Meister Eckhart was born in 1260 in the village of Hochheim in the German Rhineland. When he was fifteen he was admitted to the novitiate of the Order of Preachers, the Dominicans, at the nearby monastery of Erfurt. After taking his vows he was sent to study at the *Studium Generale* in Cologne where, possibly, he met St Albert, the "great" Dominican theologian. In 1293 he studied in Paris for the first time.

In 1294 he was elected Prior of his old Convent at Erfurt, and in 1300 he had the great honour of being elected to study again at the *Studium Generale* of St Jacques where, in 1302, he was awarded his Licentiate and Master's degree at the university of Paris. From then onwards he was known as Meister Eckhart.

In 1303 he was elected Provincial of the Saxon province, in 1307 he became Vicar of Bohemia, and in 1313 he was appointed Professor of Theology, Prior, Spiritual Director and Preacher at Strasbourg. He was also in charge of the ring of Dominican convents surrounding Strasbourg, and it was here that his reputation as a preacher was built. He preached in the vernacular rather than in Latin, and has been called the "father of modern German". In 1322 he became Regent Master of the *Studium Generale* at Cologne, the former chair of St Albert the Great.

In 1325 the Dominicans in Venice heard with consternation rumours that one of their brethren in Germany was "setting forth things in his sermons to the common people that might easily lead his listeners into error". The reason for their fears was the spreading influence in the Rhineland of wild, mystic groups and societies which were not prepared to submit to the authority of the Church.

Eckhart replied: "If the ignorant are not taught they will never learn, and none of them will ever know the art of living and dying. The ignorant are taught in the hope of changing them from ignorant to enlightened people."

However, in 1327 he was required to appear before the Franciscan Archbishop of Cologne to answer charges of heresy. His answer was that "I may err but I may not be a heretic – for the first has to do with the mind and the second with the will". (Blakney, Harper and Row, 1941). He was then, as always, loyal and obedient to the Church, but the charges against him were not dropped; in 1327 he appealed to Rome and started to walk the five hundred miles to Avignon to plead his case at the papal court. The time and place of his death is uncertain but it occurred before March 1329 when the Papal Bull was issued which condemned some of his propositions as heretical. He, himself, was never declared a heretic.

I am thankful that so little is known of Eckhart's life or of his personality. Scholastics are free to argue about whether or not he was a "mystic" (whatever that may mean – it is a word he never used and he never described visionary experiences). We have been spared, too, psychological assessments of his life, and also his representation, real or imaginary, in "holy" pictures, the like of which have damaged the image of so many saints in our history. I do not want to know what he looked like. It is not the outward appearance but what he said that makes him so important. But I am sure that Meister Eckhart laughed, that he was neither "pious" nor pompous, and that he enjoyed his life and his search for God. He was no solitary visionary. Many of the jobs he had in the Order were administrative. His life must have been both busy and practical.

I was directed to Eckhart's teaching by Marco Pallis, musician, author and mountaineer, when I first met him in 1951. Although a cradle Catholic I had given up the practice of my religion after my father's death when I was fifteen. I roamed around for six years in an unhappy limbo, looking for the answers to questions about life and death which were evaded by all the religious I talked to. After reading his book *Peaks and Lamas*, which discusses Tibetan Buddhism, I asked Marco Pallis how it could be possible to be reasonably intelligent and also a Christian when no one seemed even to admit that there were questions to ask. I was always told to go home and say my prayers and to pray for faith particularly. In fact, my faith, except in the reality of God's existence, was gone, not of my own volition but from lack of understanding.

Marco said, "Go back to the religion of your birth. Go to the Sacraments. Read Eckhart." I did all that he said. At first when I read Meister Eckhart I was bewildered, but I liked what I read and I knew that this man held the answers I wanted to find. I went back to Marco and said, "I like him but I only understand fragments of what he is saying". Marco said, "Don't try to understand him. Just go on reading him". So I did. And now every time I read again what I have read before I understand a little better. I will never understand him fully. To do so I would need to be as saintly as he was; but I continue to learn.

*

Marco Pallis, who is not a Catholic, has continually

pressed on me the need for having the condemnation of Meister Eckhart's teachings rescinded so that they would become more widely read. In 1980, Father Simon Tugwell O.P., to whom I am deeply grateful, agreed to put a petition to the General Chapter meeting of the Dominicans in Warleburg if sufficient evidence of support could be produced. Eminent people, some religious some lay, from different religions, signed the petition, as well as the Dominican Regents of Studies in England and Ireland, the Provincials of England and Ireland, and the Mother General of the Irish Dominican Sisters, requesting the General Chapter to ask the Sacred Congregation for the Faith to "examine the possibility of issuing an official declaration of the orthodoxy of Meister Eckhart and rescinding the condemnation of his teaching contained in the Bull *In agro dominico* 27 March 1329.

"The reasons for this request are:
1. that there appears now to be a scholarly consensus that his teaching is not heretical;
2. that there is growing interest in Eckhart both inside and outside the Church;
3. that the condemnation gives scandal to sincere people outside the Catholic church, both other Christians and members of non-Christian religions;
4. that Eckhart already plays a considerable role in the dialogue between Christians and Eastern non-Christian religions, and it needs to be made clear whether he is acceptable to the Church as a Christian theologian and spiritual master.

"Clearly it would be necessary to request scholars and theologians to re-examine the corpus of Eckhart's writing with a view to establishing his orthodoxy", etc.

The petition was agreed at the General Chapter, almost with unanimity, and in May 1983 the Master General of the Dominicans instituted the Eckhart Commission, appointing most eminent scholars who, in 1986, reported their findings to the Master General.

They suggested an official declaration by the Pope, acknowledging the exemplary character of Eckhart's activity and preaching (especially in his exercise of the *cure monialum*) and recommending his writings (particularly the spiritual works, treatises and sermons) as an expression of authentic Christian mysticism and as trustworthy guides to Christian life according to the spirit of the Gospel.

Such a declaration would without doubt:

a) be appreciated by numerous scholars of mediaeval mysticism;

b) promote dialogue with experts on the mystical traditions of other religions;

c) encourage many sisters and brothers of the Order of Preachers to read and study the writings of Eckhart, as well as the other eminent representatives of the mystical tradition in the Order;

d) encourage many lay people to read and meditate the spiritual writings of Meister Eckhart (the petition addressed to the Chapter at Warleberg in 1980 was, in fact, the result of initiatives taken by lay people and friends of the Order acquainted with Eckhart and Rhineland mystics).

The Commission is also preparing the draft for "a *Supplicatio* to be addressed by the Master General to the Pope, requesting a positive declaration on Eckhart's teaching and writings".

In September 1985 one hundred and fifty participants in the seminar on the "Ecclesial mission of Adrienne von Speyr" were received in audience by Pope John Paul II. In his discourse to them (quoted in *L'Osservatore Romano*, 28 October 1985) the Holy Father said, "I am very pleased with your work. Together you have sought to discern better the mysterious and impressive action of the Lord in a human existence thirsting for him. In saying that, doubtlessly because Adrienne von Speyr is Swiss, I think of the marvellous history of Rheno-Flemish mysticism of the thirteenth and especially the fourteenth centuries . . . Finally, I rejoice because the Church always needs to propose the example of laity at one and the same time rooted in their socio-professional vocation and immersed in God. Did not Eckhart teach his disciples: 'All that God asks you most pressingly is to go out of yourself . . . and let God be God in you'? (cf. *Tracts and Sermons*). One could think that in separating himself from creatures, the mystic leaves his brothers, humanity, behind. The same Eckhart affirms that, on the contrary, the mystic is marvellously present to them, on the only level where he can truly reach them, that is in God".

And so, although the fight for the official rehabilitation of Meister Eckhart will continue, for practical purposes his rehabilitation has already been accomplished.

GLOSSARY

Eckhart's Definitions

God

God is a light shining in itself in silent stillness.

God is such that we apprehend him better by negation than affirmation.

God is a word, an unspoken word.

The Eternal Birth

Birth must be taken in the sense of revelation, the Son being said to be born of the Father because he reveals the Father as father.

Essence

Essence is self-absorbed: not an effusion but an inner fusion.

Nature

Nature is the thing that essence can receive.

The Multitude

The powers of the soul and their works, memory, understanding and will, these are the multitude, these all diversify you.

21

Unity

Unity unifies multiplicity but multiplicity unites not unity.

Union

Binding and knitting together, that is the meaning of union.

Union postulates likeness.

In one God is found, so to find God a man must be one.

The Powers of the Soul

The powers of the soul and their works, memory, understanding and will, these are the multitude, these will diversify you.

The Soul's Perfection

The soul's perfection consists in liberation from life which is in part an admission to the life which is whole.

Perfection

The essence of perfection lies in bearing poverty, misery, despising, adversity and every hardship that befalls, willingly, gladly, freely, eagerly, calm and unmoved and persisting unto death without a why.

The Soul

In her actuality she is, like the Father, making all things new.

The soul is simply the motionless form of the body.

The Divine Light

With divine light the natural life is no obstacle to the eternal light, or, in other words, there is no consenting to sin . . . knowledge with the power to apply it, that is the eternal light.

Knowledge

Knowledge is power.

Unknowing

This is transformed knowledge, not ignorance which comes from lack of knowing.

The Just Man

The just man serves neither God nor creature; he is free; and the more he is just the more he is free and the more he is freedom itself.

The good man wants no praise, he wants to be praiseworthy.

Just Men

One sign of them is that they are warm; there is no half-heartedness, tardiness or disinclination in them to good works.

The Unjust Man

The further off he is from God the more stagnant and cold and insipid he will be.

Eternal Happiness

The kernel of the prime conception of eternal happiness is knowledge.

Potential Intellect

The mind is active when it is functioning, in the other [case] receptive, when God takes up the work and then the mind ought, nay must, remain still and allow God to act. Before this is begun by the mind and finished by God the spirit has prevision of it, potential knowledge of its happening. This is the meaning of potential intellect.

Will

Will as will is not receptive, not in any wise; will consists in aspiration.

Truth

That is truth which reveals what I have in my heart without likeness.

Truth is a most noble thing. If God were able to backslide from truth I would fain cling to truth and let God go. But God is truth and things in time, the things God created, are not truth.

Obedience

True and perfect obedience is the virtue of virtues.

Beauty

St Dionysius says that beauty is good order with pre-eminent lucidity.

Perception

Perception here means seeing in the light that is in time.

Freedom

A heathen philosopher says, "That thing is free which cleaves to naught and to which naught cleaves". So there is nothing free but the first cause, that is the cause of all things.

Rest

St Augustine says rest is complete lack of motion; body and soul bereft of their own nature.

Opposites

What are opposites? Good and bad, white and black are in opposition, a thing which has no place in real being.

Sin

Sin is born of negation.

Hell

Hell torment really means the frequent lapsing of the soul from the purpose of God's effort, which is to bring the soul to life again.

Grace

Grace is God's agent of mercy.

Prayer

Prayer is the practice of pure being and glorying therein.

Life

What is life? God's existence is my life.

God

The nature of God is beyond anything that man can conceive. Augustine says "All scripture is vain" when it tries to describe God.

Eckhart, in the following passages, says that God is "a light shining in itself"; that he is manifest neither in time nor place; that he is an unspoken word; he is causeless, with no before or after; he is neither being nor goodness nor spirit.

It is no good trying to understand this by using reason, for what could be the rational meaning of a paradox? What is an "unspoken word"? Or how can anything be causeless? God is not a "thing" nor has he a "body". He is neither form nor matter. Trying to stretch our minds to reasoning out beyond the limits of reason is a forlorn task. We have to accept that what Eckhart, supported by the community of saints, says is true, not straining to reason it out but letting the truth become apparent of itself. So naming God can only be an attempt to give him a "form", to make him manifest in a way which will reduce him to the level of human concepts. The brother says that by naming God "thou art abasing him".

*

"Man's best chance of finding God is where he left him." *Man's nature is such that, whatever he may seem to be doing or however far he may seem to be from the mark, he is really searching for God.*

27

1

God

The Nature of God

God is a light shining in itself in silent stillness. (p.146)

God is not in any place . . . God is not here, or there not in time or place. (p.92)

God is better than anything we can conceive; I say, God is somewhat, I know not what, verily I know not. He is all that is being rather than not being, existent more than non-existent; our highest aspirations are but grovelling things falling hopelessly short of God. He transcends heart's desire. (p.133)

God does not see in time nor is his outlook subject to renewal. (p.495)

God is a word, an unspoken word. Augustine says: "All scripture is vain". We say that God is unspoken, but he is unspeakable. Grant he is somewhat: who can pronounce this word? None but the word. God is the word which pronounces itself. Where God exists he is saying this word; where he does not exist he says nothing. God is spoken and unspoken. The Father is the speaking energy and the Son is the speech energizing. What is in me goes forth of me; I have but to think, and my word goes forth, at the same time abiding within. Even so does the Father speak forth his Son who meanwhile remains within him unspoken. I have repeatedly said, God's exit is his entrance. (pp.68-70)

This nature is causeless, therefore it is unfathomable except to causeless understanding. Creaturely intelligence is finite, so it has a cause; hence it cannot fathom causeless mind, not Christ nor his humanity. Where God is beholding his own nature which is groundless, it is incomprehensible except to groundless understanding. This understanding is none other than his nature in itself: only God in his own nature can conceive himself. This conception is the understanding wherein, self-revealed, God manifests in light that no man can attain to. (p.95)

God is everything good in all and he possesses himself in all, for what God is he is in all. When a man says he has love and wisdom and will and goodness, he is that, for God is that. God is not naught. God was before naught. God has no before and no after: naught has a sequel, its sequel is aught. Naught's fore is God, for he is before naught, and naught's after is aught. God none goes before, none comes after. Lo, the cause of all things, poised in itself in the invisible light which is himself! God is a light self-poised in absolute stillness. (p.190 Book 2)

God is not being nor yet goodness. Goodness cleaves to being and does not go beyond it: if there were no being there would be no goodness. (p.211)

We say that God is a spirit. Not so. If God were really a spirit he would be spoken. According to St Gregory, we cannot rightly speak of God at all. Anything we say of him is bound to be a stammering. (p.104)

If God were able to backslide from truth I would fain cling to truth and let God go.

Naming God

There is no knowing what God is. Something we do know, namely, what God is not. (p.18)

I hold it is as wrong for me to say that God is being as to say the sun is black or white. God is neither this nor that. (p.211)

In God is no good nor better nor best. To say that God is good is to do him wrong: as well say that the sun is black. (p.211)

We hear of one good man who in prayers besought God for his name. Then, "Peace!" quoth a brother, "thou art abasing God." (p.70)

Among names none is more appropriate than He-who-is. That one should recognize a thing and simply say it is, would seem absurd; call it a stone, a bit of wood, and we know what that means. But suppose everything detached, abstracted, pared away, and nothing left except the IS; that is the characteristic nature of his name. (p.83)

Philosophers say that out of the summit of the soul there flow twin powers. The one will the other intellect, and her powers' perfection lies in the sovran power of intellect. This never rests. It wants God not as Holy Ghost nor yet as Son; it flees the Son. It wants God not as God. And why? Because thus he has name; were there a thousand Gods yet would it penetrate them all in the desire to get to where he has no name at all: it wants a nobler, better thing than God as having name. (p.43)

The Search for God

All creatures are by nature endeavouring to be like God. The heavens would not revolve unless they followed on the track of God or of his likeness. If God were not in all things, nature would stop dead, not working and not wanting. (p.115)

All creatures are crying aloud to man, "You look for truth and goodness which we are not: seek God, he is both truth and goodness." Man is always searching for holiness and happiness. (p.168 Book 2)

Whether you sleep or wake God goes on with his work. That we have no sense of it is because our tongue is furred with the slime of creatures and does not possess the salt of divine affection. (p.224)

What is required of a man to dwell in God? He requires three things. First, to renounce himself and all things, not cleaving to aught that is grasped by the senses within nor abiding in any creature existing in time or in eternity. Again, he must love neither this nor that good; he must love good for good's sake, since nothing is good or desirable except in so far as God is therein. (p.156)

I once said and it is very true: When a man goes out of himself to find God or fetch God, he is wrong. I do not find God outside myself nor conceive him excepting as my own and in me. (p.163)

I sometimes say, beginners of the virtuous life should do as he does who describes a circle; the starting point once fixed, he keeps it so and then the trace is good. In other words, learn first to fix the heart on God, on good and on good works. (p.158)

It is a law of nature that fluids run downhill into anything adapted to receive them; the higher not receiving from the lower but the lower from the higher. Now God is higher than the soul and hence there is a constant flow of God into the soul which cannot miss her. The soul may well miss it but as long as man keeps right under God he immediately catches this divine influence straight out of God. Nor is he subject to anything else, nor fear nor pain nor pleasure nor anything that is not God. (p.235)

All God wants of you is for you to go out of yourself in respect of your creatureliness and let God be God in you. (p.49)

To see God needs high aspiration. Know, ardent desire and abject humility work wonders. I vow God is omnipotent, but he is impotent to thwart the humble soul with towering aspiration. . . . I say, and I would stake my life upon it, that by will a man might pierce a wall of steel, and accordingly we read about St Peter that on catching sight of Jesus he walked upon the water in his eagerness to meet him. (p.133)

Man's best chance of finding God is where he left him. As it was with you when you last had him, so let it be now while you have lost him, then you will find him. Good will never loses, never misses God at any time. People often say, we have good will. Theirs is not God's will though; they want to have their own way and dictate to God to do so and so. That is not good will. We must find out from God what his will is. Broadly speaking, what God wills is that we should give up willing. (pp.15-16 Book 2)

On no account let anyone suppose that he is far from God because of his infirmities or faults or for any other reason. If at any time your great shortcomings make an outcast of you and you cannot take yourself as being near to God, take it then at any rate that he is near to you, for it is most mischievous to set God at a distance. Man goes far away or near but God never goes far off; he is always standing close at hand, and even if he cannot stay within he goes no further than the door. (p.23 Book 2)

He who fondly imagines to get more of God in thoughts, prayers, pious offices and so forth, than by the fireside and in the stall: in sooth he does but take God, as it were, and swaddle his head in a cloak and hide him under the table. For he who seeks God under settled forms lays hold of the form while missing the God concealed in it. But he who seeks God in no special guise lays hold of him as he is in himself and such an one, "lives with the Son" and is the life itself. (p.49)

Man should not be afraid of God. Some fear is harmful. The right sort of fear is the fear of losing God. (p.223)

God's Love

If anyone should ask me what God is, I should answer: God is love, and so altogether lovely that creatures all with one accord essay to love his loveliness, whether they do so knowingly or unbeknownst, in joy or sorrow. (p.26)

"God is love." That is so inasmuch as all that can love, all that does love, he compels by his love to love him. God is love, secondly, inasmuch as every God-created and loving thing compels him by its love to love it, willy-nilly. God is love, thirdly, inasmuch as his love drives all his lovers out of multiplicity. The love of God in multiplicity pursues the love which is himself right out of multiplicity into his very unity.

God is love, fourthly, who by his love provides all creatures with their life and being, preserving them in his love. The colour of the cloth is preserved in the cloth: even so creatures are preserved in existence by love, that is God. Take the colour from cloth, its subsistence is gone: so do creatures all lose their subsistence if taken from love, to wit, God. God is love, and so lovely is he that lovers all love him, willy-nilly. No creature is so vile as to love what is bad. What we love must be good or must seem to be good. But creaturely good, all told, is rank evil as compared with God. St Augustine says, "Love, that in meditating love thou mayst provide the wherewithal to satisfy thy soul". God is love. (p.25)

"God is love, and he who dwells in love dwells in God and God in him." There is a difference between ghostly things and bodily things. One ghostly thing dwells in another; but nothing bodily dwells in another. There may be water in a tub, with the tub round it. But where the wood is the water is not. In this sense no material thing dwells in another. But spiritual things dwell in each other: each several angel with all his joy and happiness is in every other angel as well as in himself, and every angel with all his joy and happiness dwells in me, and God to boot with his entire beatitude, though I discern it not. (p.26)

God longs as urgently for you to go out of yourself in respect of your creaturely nature as though his whole felicity depended on it. (p.50)

I never give God thanks for loving me, because he cannot help it. . . . What I do thank him for is not being able of his goodness to leave off loving me. (p.179)

God loves my soul so much that his very life and being depend upon his loving me, whether he would or no. To stop God loving me would be to rob him of his Godhood; for God is love no less than he is truth; as he is good so is he love as well. (p.26)

True and perfect love is shown by having lively hope and trust in God. There is no better proof of love than trust. Wholehearted love for another must imply trust, and with God all we dare to expect does really come true, and a thousandfold more. And just as we can never love God too much so neither can we ever put too much faith in him. Of all things a man can do nothing is so seemly as putting trust in God. Not one of those who ever had great confidence in God did he ever fail; he wrought great things with them. For well he knew that this faith always comes from love, though faith is not the only thing love has; it has actual knowledge, absolute certainty. (p.20 Book 2)

Love does not unite, not in any wise. Satisfaction (or enough) is not what holds together, binds together. Love unites in act and not in essence. . . . Neither knowledge nor love unites anything. Love takes God only as being good and God escapes from name. Good, love goes no further than that. Love takes God under a veil, under a garment.

God's Forgiveness

Where there are sins there is no perfect trust or love; but love entirely masks sin; it has no sense of sin. Not that no sins have been committed, but suddenly they are blotted out and vanish as though they had not been. God's works are all done suddenly, abundantly: whom he forgives he forgives outright and altogether and rather much than little as becomes entire trust. (p.21 Book 2)

As God Loves all of us so We
should Love all our Neighbours

We know of three kinds of love that our Lord had, and in this we must be like him. One is natural, the second gracious and the third divine. In God there is nothing not God; in ourselves, however, we may consider them as an ascending scale, from good to better and from better to perfection. But in God is neither more nor less, he is just the simple, pure, essential truth. The first love God has, in this we learn how his divine goodness has constrained him to create all creatures, wherewith he has been big eternally in his ideal preconception, intending them to enjoy his goodness with him. And among all his creatures he bears no more love to one than to another: as each is able to receive he pours his love therein. Were my soul as capacious, as roomy, as a Seraph's, who has nothing in him, God would pour out into me the same as he does into that angel. If you describe a circle, a ring of dots with one point in the middle, from this point all the dots will be equidistant; for one dot to get nearer it will have to be displaced, for the middle point is constant at the centre. So with divine being: it is not questing round about but abiding altogether in itself. In order to receive from it a creature must infallibly be moved out of itself. And when we talk of man we are talking of all creatures; Christ himself exhorted his disciples, "Go forth and preach the Gospel to all creatures", for creatures all culminate in man. Not but what, as being, God is pouring himself out into all creatures, to each as much as it can take. Which is a lesson to us to love all creatures equally with what we have received from God (though some are nearer to us by kinship or natural friendship), as we are favoured equally with the boon of divine love. I sometimes seem to like one better than another, and yet I have the same good will towards that other person whom I have never seen, only, by asking more of me, this one enables me to give myself more. God loves creatures all alike and fills them with his being. And we too should pour forth ourselves in love upon all creatures. We often find the heathen arriving at this amiable state in virtue of their natural understanding. As the heathen philosopher observes, man is by nature a kindly animal. (pp.214-15)

Method

"Why is it, Meister Eckhart, that people are so slow to look for God in earnest?"

"When one is looking for a thing and finds no trace of its existence one hunts half-heartedly and in distress. But, lighting on some vestige of the quarry, the chase grows lively, blithe and keen. The man in quest of fire, cheered when he feels the heat, looks for its source with eagerness and pleasure. And so it is with those in quest of God: feeling none of the sweetness of God they grow listless but, sensing the sweetness of divinity, they blithely pursue their search for God."

*

Meister Eckhart says that the man who finds no taste of God wearies of looking for him. One of the criticisms of Christianity, and one of the reasons why many young Christians turn to the East, to Buddhism or to Hinduism, is that in Christianity there is no apparent help with method. How do we find God? How do we even start?

Eckhart is one of the Christians who faces this and accepts it as a problem. Good intentions are not always enough. We need instruction in how to make ourselves fit to receive the revelation of God, to receive the eternal birth.

The eternal birth, he says, is like "making holiday, learning to be happy, to be free from care.

"Before this birth can happen we must be at peace, not fragmented by worldly distractions but united and in harmony within, like the sound of a major chord."

By withdrawing from the world (which does not mean isolating oneself from it or becoming unconcerned about it. It means having no self-interest, becoming sufficiently detached to be wise), we discover the essence of the soul. Like the eye of a hurricane it is still and silent and with no activity. The "powers" of the soul, the intellect, the memory, the will or the powers of the senses, emanate from the essence but they are swirling in constant activity while the essence is always still.

Usually we learn by taking in knowledge through our senses from the world around us, but this birth wells up from within and reverses the process of knowing. We know from within and not from without so sometimes it is called an "unknowing".

We survive each day by using powers of reason. "Because the sun has risen every day of my life it is reasonable to suppose it will rise again tomorrow" and I plan accordingly. Reason clings to thoughts of survival, to tangible signs from the world around, making what sense and whatever pattern it can from them. We try to reduce God also to a pattern, to a "being", which can be analysed and divided into qualities and quantities, as we do when we reason. But we cannot divide up naught, and God is beyond and before naught. Rational thinking can only bypass God or, alternatively, produce a figment of imagination, an image claiming, "This must be God". The eternal birth is God revealing himself to the man who "hews out and brings to light the divine form which God has wrought into his nature".

It is a process of "letting go", letting go of the soul powers, intellect, memory, will, the senses, to achieve the freedom and the stillness to "wait upon God".

We have to work to prepare ourselves but we do not have to worry. God does the work in us as long as we are willing to be worked upon. By letting go of all distractions *we prepare the ground for a focus of attention which, like deepening a river to strengthen its force, provides the power to reach out beyond reason towards God.*

Letting go leads not to torpor but to strength. It is the stripping away of anything which diverts or fragments. It is the first step on the road towards that state of "potential receptivity" in which the Son is born. Reaching this state requires self-training. When the mind is free to listen to God, the body relaxed and the demands of the senses stilled, we see God in one single image.

2

Method

The Eternal Birth

Making Holiday – learning to be happy

Here in time we make holiday because the eternal birth
which God the Father bore and bears unceasingly in eternity is now born in time, in human nature. St Augustine
says this birth is always happening. But if it happens not in
me what does it profit me? (p.3)

The Preparation

The soul in which this birth shall come to pass must be
absolutely pure and must live in gentle fashion, quite
peacefully and wholly introverted: not running out
through the five senses into the manifoldness of creatures
but altogether within and harmonized in her summit. That
is its place. Anything inferior is disdained by it. (p.3)

Silence

. . . It is bound to be in the purest part of the soul, in the
noblest, in her ground, aye, in the very essence of the soul.
That is mid-silence for thereunto no creature did ever get,
nor any image, nor has the soul there either activity or
understanding, therefore she is not aware of any image
either of herself or any creature. Whatever the soul effects
she effects with her powers. When she understands she
understands with her intellect. When she remembers she

40

does so with her memory. When she loves she does so with her will, she works then with her powers and not with her essence. Now every exterior act is linked with some means. The power of seeing is brought into play only through the eyes; elsewhere she can neither do nor bestow such a thing as seeing. And so with all the other senses; their operations are always effected through some means or other. But there is no activity in the essence of the soul; the faculties she works with emanate from the ground of the essence but in her actual ground there is mid-stillness; here alone is rest and a habitation for this birth, this act wherein God the Father speaks his word, for it is intrinsically receptive of naught save the divine essence, without means. (p.4)

No one can experience this birth without a mighty effort. None can attain this birth unless he can withdraw his mind entirely from things. And it requires main force to drive back all the senses and inhibit them. Violence must be offered to them one and all or this cannot be done. (p.14)

The Mind is still when it stops Thought and goes beyond Time

This birth transcends here and now. "Here", that is place; "now" that is time. It befalls in eternity. (p.77)

First of all when a word is conceived in my mind it is a subtle, intangible thing; it is true word when it takes shape in my thought. Later, as spoken aloud by my mouth, it is but outward expression of the interior word. Even so the eternal Word is spoken in the innermost and purest recesses of the soul, in the summit of her rational nature, and there befalls this birth. (p.80)

To still your Mind you must still your Body too

If you will find this noble birth, truly you must quit the multitude and return to the starting-point, into the ground out of which you have come. The powers of the soul and their works, these are the multitude: memory, understanding and will, these all diversify you, therefore you must leave them all: sensible perception, imagination and everything wherein you find yourself and have yourself in view. Thereafter you may find this birth, but, believe me, not otherwise. (pp.20-1)

The Kingdom of God is within you. Don't look for help from outside, or strain to reason

Now the question arises, whether this birth is to be found in anything which, albeit relating to God, is nevertheless taken in from without through the senses, in any presentment of God as good, wise or compassionate, or whatever intellect can conceive of divinity: whether this birth is to be found in such-like things? In truth, no! For, although good and god-like, they are nevertheless introduced from without through the senses; all must well up from within, out of God, if this birth is to shine with a really clear light, and your own work must lie over, every faculty serving his ends not your own. If this work is to be done, God alone must do it, and you must undergo it. Where from your willing and knowing you truly go out, God with his knowing surely and willingly goes in and shines there clearly. Where God thus knows himself your knowledge is of no avail and cannot stand. Do not fondly imagine that your reason can grow to the knowledge of God; that God shall shine in you divinely no natural light can help to bring about; it must be utterly extinguished and go out of itself altogether, then God can shine in with his light bringing back with him everything you went out of and a thousand more, besides the new form containing it all. (p.21)

No sooner does a man know the reason of a thing than immediately he tires of it and goes casting about for something new. Always clamouring to know, he is ever inconstant. The soul is constant only to this unknowing knowing which keeps her pursuing. (p.7)

The Eternal Birth is constant Revelation

How is God ever being born in man? Look you, suppose a man hews out and brings to light the divine form which God has wrought into his nature, then God's image in him stands revealed. Birth must be taken in the sense of revelation, the Son being said to be born of the Father, because he reveals the Father as Father. So the more and more clearly God's image shows in man, the more evidently God is born in him. And by God's eternal birth in him we understand that his image stands fully revealed . . . this man is ever being born in God. How can a man ever be born in God? Lo! by revealing this form in a man the man grows like unto God, for the form of man is the same as the image of God which is God in every respect. The more he is like God the more he is one. So man's eternal birth in God we understand to mean ideal man refulgent in God's image. (pp.156-7)

Let Go

You must know that God is born in us as soon as all our soul-powers, which hitherto have been tied and bound, are absolutely free (and passive) and when the mind is stilled and sense troubles us no longer. (p.151)

When does this Birth happen?

Regarding this birth there arises the question, Does it happen continuously or only at intervals when one is disposed for it, what time one is exerting oneself to the utmost to forget things altogether and be conscious in this?
     . . . since the uninterrupted vision and passion of God is

intolerable to the soul in this body, therefore God with-draws from the soul from time to time, as it is said, "A little while ye see me, and again a little while and ye do not see me". (pp.14-15)

Preparation

"I must be about my Father's business." This text is opportune to what we have to say concerning the eternal birth which took place here in time and is still happening daily in the innermost recesses of the soul, in her ground, remote from all comers. To become aware of this interior birth it is above all necessary to be about my Father's business. (p.14)

Concentration and Recollection

Don't Worry

A city is something enclosed and centred within. And so must the soul be whereinto God flows. She must be safe from outside alarms, her forces assembled within. (p.158)

Let God operate in you; hand the work over to him and don't worry (disquiet yourself) as to whether or no he is working with nature or above nature, for his are both nature and grace. What business is it of yours what it suits him to work with or what he is doing with you or with anyone else? (p.41 Book 2)

He that would be what he ought must stop being what he is. (p.423)

Let Go

To know ourselves, to be installed in God, this is not hard seeing that God himself must be working in us; for it is godly work: man acquiescing and making no resistance; he is passive while allowing God to act in him. (p.179)

He who is everywhere at home is Godworthy; to him who is ever the same is God present, and in him in whom creatures are stilled God bears his one-begotten Son. (p.418)

The more recollected the soul the less scattered she is, and the more concentrated the wider her ken. (p.89)

Go into training

We must learn to act without attachment. But it is rare for anyone untrained to reach the stage at which he is proof against disturbance by any act or any body. This needs prodigiously hard work; and for God to be as present and to show as plainly to him at all times and in all company, that is for the expert and demands especially two things. One is that the man be closeted within himself where his mind is safe from images of outside things which remain external to him and, alien as they are, cannot traffic or forgather with him or find any room in him at all. Secondly, inventions of the mind itself, ideas, spontaneous notions or images of things outside or whatever comes into his head, he must give no quarter to on pain of scattering himself and being sold into multiplicity. His powers must all be trained to turn and face his inner self. (p.31 Book 2)

Here, the soul is scattered abroad among her powers and dissipated in the act of each; the power of seeing in the eye, the power of hearing in the ear, the power of tasting in the tongue, and her powers are accordingly enfeebled for their interior work, scattered forces being imperfect. It follows that, for her interior work to be effective, she must call in all her powers, recollecting them out of extended things to one interior act. (pp.11-12)

When do the passions perforce obey the mind? The answer Meister Eckhart gives is this. What time the mind is fixed on God and there abides, the senses are obedient to the mind. As one should hang a needle to a magnet, and then another needle onto that, until there are four needles, say, depending from the magnet. As long as the first needle stays clinging to the magnet all the other needles will keep clinging on to that, but when the leader drops the rest will go as well. So, while the mind keeps fixed on God the senses are subservient to it, but if the mind should wander off from God, the passions will escape and be unruly. (p.426)

It behoves us to withdraw from things in order to concentrate our powers on perceiving and knowing the one infinite and immortal truth! To this end assemble your entire mind and memory: turn them into the ground where your treasure lies hidden. But for this you must drop all other activities; you must get to unknowing to find it. (p.12)

The saints behold God in a simple image and in that image they discern all things; and God himself sees himself thus, perceiving all things in himself. He need not turn, as we do, from one thing to another. Supposing that in this life we were always confronted by a mirror wherein we see and recognize all things at a glance in one single image: neither act nor knowledge would be a hindrance then. At present we must turn from one thing to another: we can only mind one thing at the expense of all the others. And the soul is bound so straitly to her powers that where they flow she must flow with them; the soul must be present at everything they do, and attentive too, or nothing would come of their exertions. (p.12)

Emptiness. Letting Go of Things

By keeping yourself empty and bare, merely tracking and following and giving up yourself to this darkness and ignorance without turning back, you may well win that which is all things. And the more you are barren of yourself and ignorant of things the nearer you are thereto. (p.22)

If the soul were stripped of all her sheaths God would be discovered all naked to her view and would give himself to her withholding nothing. As long as the soul has not thrown off all her veils, however thin, she is unable to see God. Any medium, but a hair's breadth, in between the body and the soul stops actual union. (p.114)

The soul must be without admixture. If someone hangs something to my cloak or sticks something on it then anyone who wears the cloak will wear too its attachments. If I go out hence, there will then go with me the whole of my attachments. What the spirit rests on, is attached to, takes the spirit with it. The man who rests on nothing, is attached to nothing, though heaven and earth should fall, will remain unmoved. (p.115)

Our Lord repays an hundredfold the man who leaves all things. Letting go all things he gets an hundredfold return and eternal life. If it happens to a man in the course of riddance to get again the very same he gave, then, not giving all, he shall get nothing. (p.140)

Such is the nature of God that we know it by nothing better than naught. How by naught? – By getting rid of all means, not merely by spurning the world and the possession of virtue: I must let virtue go if I would see God face to face; not that I should flout virtue, but virtue being innate in me I transcend virtue. When a man's mind has lost touch with everything then, not till then, it comes in touch with God. (p.144)

Escaping Multiplicity

How can we be perfectly simple? By departing from things and from ourselves, and knowing our own mind and all the working of the powers of the soul, except the chief one, understanding: leave that to God alone. The passive soul stands to lose all this and leave God to work without hindrance; then he begets his perfect likeness in her and conforms her to himself. Then she understands with him and loves with him. This is perfection. (p.147)

God is born in us as soon as all our soul-powers, which hitherto have been tied and bound, are absolutely free (and passive) and when the mind is stilled and sense troubles us no longer. (p.151)

Abandonment to the Divine Providence

Likewise I say about the man who has brought himself to naught in himself, in God and in all creatures. That man assumes the lowest place and God is bound to empty himself whole into his soul, else would he not be God. I warrant you by God's eternal truth, that into any man who is brought low God pours out his whole self in all his might, so utterly that neither of his life, his being, nor his nature, nay, nor of his perfect Godhead, does he keep aught back, he empties out the whole thereof as fruits into that wight who in abandonment to God assumes the lowest place. (p.152)

Wherefore if you will, God and the universe are yours. That is, if you will put off self and things, doff the habit of your personality and take yourself in your divinity. (p.236)

Would you be very Christ and God? Put off, then, whatever the eternal Word did not put on. The eternal Word never put on a person. So do you strip yourself of everything personal and selfish and keep just your bare humanity. (p.236)

To hear God's Word demands absolute self-surrender. Hearer and heard are one in the eternal Word. (p.238)

He who knows one matter in all things remains unmoved. For matter is the subject of form and there can be no matter without form nor form devoid of matter. Form without matter is nothing at all; but matter ever cleaves to form and is one undivided whole in every single part of it. Now since form in itself is naught therefore it moves nothing. And since matter is perfectly impartible, therefore it is unmoved. This man, then, is unmoved by form or matter and is therefore objectless in time. (p.123)

When you have emptied yourself entirely of your own self and all things and of every sort of selfishness, and have transferred, united and abandoned yourself to God in perfect faith and complete amity, then everything that is born in you, external or internal, joyful or sorrowful, sour or sweet, is no longer your own at all, but is altogether your God's to whom you have abandoned yourself. (p.18)

Meister Eckhart said, I never ask God to give himself to me: I beg him to purify, to empty, me. If I am empty, God of his very nature is obliged to give himself to me. (p.420)

The Virgin Wife

The Doctor says, I sometimes think of what the angel said to Mary, "Hail full of grace!" What is the good to me of Mary's being full of grace if I am not full also? What does it profit me the Father's giving his Son birth unless I bear him too? (p.216)

"Our Lord went up into a certain fastness and was received by a certain virgin who was a wife."

Mark the term. Needs must it be a virgin by whom Jesus is received. Virgin is, in other words, a person void of alien images, free as he was when he existed not. It may be questioned: Man born and launched on rational life, how can he be as free from images as he was when he was not, he knowing a variety of things, images all of them: how possibly can he be void thereof? I answer that, were I sufficiently intelligent to have within me intellectually the sum of all forms conceived by man and which subsist in God himself, I having no property in them and no idea of ownership, positive or negative, past or to come, but standing in the present *now* perfectly free in the will of God and doing it perpetually: then, truly, I were a virgin, unhandicapped by forms, just as I was when I was not . . . (p.35)

Now lay this fact to heart: the ever virgin is never fruitful. To be fruitful the soul must be wife. Spouse is the noblest title of the soul, nobler than virgin. For a man to receive God within him is good, and in receiving he is virgin. But for God to be fruitful in him is still better: the fruits of his gift being gratitude therefor, and in this new-born thankfulness the spirit is the spouse bearing Jesus back into his Father's heart. (p.35)

I say: had Mary not borne God in ghostly fashion first, he never had been born of her in flesh. The woman said to Christ, "Blessed is the womb that bare thee." To which Christ replied, "Blessed not only the womb which bare me: blessed are they that hear the word of God and keep it." It is worth more to God his being brought forth ghostly in the individual virgin or good soul than that he was born of Mary bodily. (p.221 Book 1)

The virgin wife, free and unbound in her affections, is ever as near God as to herself. She abounds in fruit and is big withal, no more nor less than God is himself. This fruit, his birth, does that virgin bear who is a wife; daily she yields her hundred- and her thousandfold, nay, numberless her labours and her fruits in that most noble ground, the very ground, to speak more plainly, wherein the Father is begetting his eternal Word: there she is big with fruit. For Jesus, light and shine of the paternal heart (according to St Paul he is the "light and splendour" of the Father's heart), this Jesus is atoned with her and she with him, she is radiant with him and shining as the one alone, as one pure brilliant light in the paternal heart. (p.36)

Humility

To see God needs high aspiration. Know, ardent desire and abject humility work wonders. I vow God is omnipotent, but he is impotent to thwart the humble soul with towering aspiration. And where I cannot master God and bend him to my will it is because I fail either in will or meekness. (p.133)

According to St Chrysostom, "To be an other than I am I must abandon that I am". This is accomplished by humility. "Nothing", says St Gregory, "gives more power than does lowliness." (p.137)

It behoves a man in all he does to turn his will in God's direction, and keeping only God in view to forge ahead without a qualm, not wondering, am I right or am I doing something wrong? If the painter had to plan out every brush-mark before he made his first he would not paint at all. And if, going to some place, we had first to settle how to put the front foot down, we should never get there. Follow your principles and keep straight on; you will come to the right place, that is the way. (p.141)

Sure proof of true humility is the fearful joy of being praised. For on coming into touch with truth and finding in himself a witness of it, a man is sensible of pleasure but fears it as a likely cause of his undoing. (p.452)

My lowliness raises up God, and the lower I humble myself the higher do I exalt God, and the higher I do exalt God the more gently and sweetly he pours into me his divine gift, his divine influx. For the higher the inflowing thing the more easy and smooth is its flow. How God is raised up on my lowliness I argue thus: the more I abase and keep myself down the higher God towers above me.

The deeper the trough the higher the crest. In just the same way, the more I abase and humble myself the higher God goes and the better and easier he pours into me his divine influx. So it is true that I exalt God by my lowliness. (p.430)

How can God mortify a man with (the man) himself? It seems as though the naughting of man means divine exaltation, for in the gospel it says, "He that humbleth himself shall be exalted".

Answer, yes and no. To humble himself is not enough. God has to do it, then he shall be exalted. Not that his abasement is one thing and his exaltation is another; the highest height of exaltation lies in the low ground of humility. (p.37 Book 2)

The Holy Ghost flows into the soul as fast as she is poured forth in humility and so far as she has gotten the capacity. He fills all the room he can find. (p.158)

Stillness

Turning and change lead nowhere: stopping we progress. (p.93)

The soul must rest in God. God cannot do divine work in the soul for in the soul things are all ruled by measure. Measure means limit, within and without. There is none of this in God's operations which are infinite. (p.120)

Stand over flowing water and you cannot see yourself. But supposing it is clear, then where it is collected and still enough for a reflection you can see your form in it. (p.118)

The first and noblest work of God is motionless, divine rest. It stands to reason that the maker of the motionless is himself unmoved. Were God not unmovable there could nothing motionless be made.

Aristotle says, "All moving things proceed from rest and from necessity and moving things are all seeking rest". Man likewise then ought to be as motionless as possible. When is a man motionless? The soul is motionless when nothing whatever can perturb her, when she is neither glad nor sad and cannot be gladdened nor yet saddened. And she must be unnecessitous. "When is she unnecessitous?" The soul is unnecessitous when she has no need to cleave to any creature, and not only no need, it is hell-pain to her to dwell upon the form of creature since there is no rest for her save in the formless form of God. (p.454)

"In all things I sought rest". . . . If I were asked to say to what end the creator has created creatures I should answer: Rest. And were I asked a second time, What are all creatures seeking so eagerly by nature? I should answer: Rest. And if a third time I were asked what the soul seeks in all her agitations, once more I should say: Rest. (p.120)

This Word lies hidden in the soul, unnoticed and beyond our ken, and were it not for rumours in the ground of hearing, we should never heed it; but all sounds and voices have to cease and silence, perfect stillness, reign. (p.95)

The end of all motion is rest. (p.170)

There is not perfect rest in intellectual vision, for in mental operations there is a certain motion of external things towards the soul, in virtue of which movement the forms of these same things are drawn into and pictured in the soul, starting a psychic motion in the *is-ness* of the soul and the real being of the things appearing in the picture; and this motion extends to the will which is not at rest any more. (p.170)

What is rest? St Augustine says rest is complete lack of motion: body and soul bereft of their own nature. (p.154)

The Senses

According to some doctors, the soul is in the heart alone. Not so; it is an error some eminent Scholastics make. The soul is whole and undivided, at once in foot and eye and in each member of the body. (p.210)

The power I see with I do not hear with, nor with my

power of hearing can I see. So with the rest of the five senses. But on the other hand, the soul exists entire in every member. (p.89)

Such are the eyes and ears and the five senses: these are the soul's ways out into the world, and by these ways the world gets back into the soul. (p.135)

There is a power in sight which is superior to the eyes set in the head and more far-reaching than the heavens and earth. This power seizes all the things that come into the eyes and bears them up into the soul. (pp.88-9)

"The hand of the Lord is with him." The hand of the Lord means the Holy Ghost, for two reasons: first because work is wrought with the hand; and next, because it is one with the arm and with the body. All human actions start in the heart, extend to the limbs, and are done by the hand; so the seat of the soul being chiefly in the heart, in the heart is the mainspring of her energies. (pp.154-5)

Soul apart from body possesses neither intellect nor will: she is one with no attendant power of speech; true, she has it in her ground, in its root as it were, but not in fact. The soul is purified in body by collecting things scattered and dispersed. The resultant of the five senses, when these are recollected, gives her a common sense wherein everything sums up to one. (p.207)

Why has my mouth, my ear, no sense of heaven? Because they are not like it. St Bernard says, "My eye is like the heavens in being round and clear and placed high in the body, nor can it brook the entry of any foreign matter." Before my eye can see the painting on the wall this must be filtered through the air, and in a still more tenuous form be borne into my fantasy, to be assimilated by my understanding. These properties, both, the soul must needs possess; and this likeness, how subtle soever it may be, with its suggestiveness, its hint of sin, soul rejects as foreign to herself. If God himself were foreign to the soul she would have none of him. What the eye perceives has to be conveyed to it by means, in images. If there were no means we should see nothing. If an angel sees another angel or anything that God has made, he does so by some means. But himself and God he sees immediately. (pp.111-12)

It is only by the senses that the soul is roused and the idea of wisdom naturally imprinted in her. Plato says, and with him St Augustine: the soul has all knowledge within, and all we can do from without is but an awakening of knowledge. (p.104)

. . . Those who live the life of the five senses never touch this food. (p.89)

My soul is undivided; also, it is entire in each member. Where my eye sees my ear does not hear. My bodily hearing and sight are engineered in the mind. Light gives my eye a sense of colour which is lacking to the soul by reasons of its being a defect. All the outward senses are alive to, if the spirit is to take it in, must be raised up by the angel: he imprints it in the upper portion of the soul. (p.93)

The Common Sense

Soul apart from body possesses neither intellect nor will: she is one with no attendant power of speech; true, she has it in her ground, in its root as it were, but not in fact. The soul is purified in body by collecting things scattered and dispersed. The resultant of the five senses, when these are recollected, gives her a common sense wherein everything sums up to one. (p.207)

One master says that in this crossing over time into the now each power of the soul will surpass itself. The five powers must pass into her collective power (or common sense), and common sense will vanish into the formless power wherein nothing forms. (p.234 Book 1)

Beyond the Senses

A master says, "God would never choose that eye or ear should sense what crowns the summit of the soul: none other than the nameless place, which is the place of all things." (p.104)

A master has said that he who sees anything does not see God. (p.93)

3

The Just Man and the Unjust Man

Sons of God

"God sent his only-begotten Son into the world", by which you are to understand not the external world: it must be taken of the inner world. As surely as the Father by his simple nature begets the Son innately, so surely he begets him in the innermost recesses of the mind, which is the inner world. (p.49)

In eternity the Father is bringing forth his Son just like himself. "The Word was with God and the Word was God": the same in the same nature. . . . Not merely is she with him and he equally with her but he is in her: the Father gives birth to his Son in the soul in the very same way as he gives him birth in eternity, and in none other. He must do, willy-nilly. The Father is begetting his Son unceasingly, and furthermore, I say, he begets me his Son, as his very own Son. (p.162)

The Two Births of Man

There are two births of man: one in the world, the other one out of the world and ghostly, in God. Would you know if your child is born and if he is naked? Whether, that is to say, you have been made God's son? If your heart is heavy, except for sin, your child is not born. In your anguish you are not yet mother: you are in labour and your hour is near. Doubt not, if you are travailing for yourself or for your friend no birth has taken place though birth is close at hand. The birth is not over until your heart is free from care: then man has the essence and nature and substance and wisdom and joy and all that God has. (p.34)

God will give birth to his Son in you whether you like it or loathe it; whether you sleep or wake God goes on with his work. That we have no sense of it is because our tongue is furred with the slime of creatures and possesses not the salt of divine affection. If we had godly love we should savour God and all the works God ever wrought, and receive all things from God and be doing the same work as he does. In this sameness we are all his only son. (p.224)

According to the scriptures, "No man knoweth the Father but the Son", and hence, if you desire to know God, you have to be not merely like the Son, you have to be the very Son himself. Some people think to see God with their eyes as they would see a cow and they expect to love him as they would love a cow. This you love for its milk and for its cheese: for its profit to yourself. Even so do they who love God with an eye to outward riches or interior consolation, not rightly loving God but their own personal advantage, I trow that any object you shall set before your mind except God in himself, how good soever it may be, is nothing but a barrier to the absolute truth. (pp.52-3)

Mark whereby we are sons of God: by having the same nature as the Son of God – How can one be the Son of God, or know it, seeing that God is not like anybody? – True, Isaias says, "To whom will ye liken God or what likeness will ye compare unto him". Since it is God's nature to be not like anyone, we must needs not be so to be the same as he is. When I contrive to see myself in naught and to see naught in me; when I succeed in rooting up and casting out everything in me, then I am free to pass into the naked being of the soul. Likes must be ousted before I can be transplanted into God and be the same as he is: same substance, same essence, same nature and the Son of God. (p.33)

The Father bears his Son in the innermost recesses of the soul and begets you with his only Son, no less. But if I am

Son then I must be Son the same as he is Son, and in no other way. If I am a man I am a man man-fashion. If I am the Man I am the Man Man-fashion. As St John says, "Ye are God's sons". (p.164)

We are all Children of God

This (Mary bearing God Ghostly-fashion) involves the notion of our being the only Son whom the Father has eternally begotten. When the Father begat all creatures he was begetting me; I flowed out with all creatures while remaining within in the Father. (p.221)

On one occasion I was asked what the Father is doing in heaven. I said, He is begetting his Son, an act he so delights in and which pleases him so well that he does nothing else but generate his Son, and these two are flowering with the Holy Ghost. When the Father gives birth to his Son in me I am his very Son and not another: we are another in manhood, true, but there I am the Son himself and no other. As sons we are lawful heirs. He who knows the truth knows this well. The word "Father" connotes just begetting and having of sons. We are sons in his Son and are the Son himself. (p.110)

The Just Man

It was a revelation to me to read that the just man, the holy man, is also, according to Eckhart, a likeable man. Looking through the pictures in the old Lives of the Saints, I see faces which I might respect, even venerate, from a distance, but whom I would never think of inviting home for supper. The "Holy" man is the dark, sombre person, speaking as though he has plums in his mouth, never laughing, isolated in his superiority. But I would love to have Eckhart home for supper. To him the just man is warm and happy and he laughs with God. The just man is the happy man. If in order to find God we have to be miserable and afraid then it's a queer kind of God we are looking for.

He warns us against dabbling in religions – taking a little from here and a little from there, as though it were from an hors d'oeuvres *tray. By deepening the knowledge of our own religion we strengthen our understanding of it and of the world.*

The Just Man

As the heathen philosopher observes, man is by nature a kindly animal. (p.215)

The Just Man is Warm

Let us see what people are dwelling in God. One sign of them is that they are warm; there is no half-heartedness, tardiness or disinclination in them to good works. We have seen . . . that the waters are not frozen at their source: that is because the sun draws the moisture from the bottom of the hill up to the top and out of the hill so that it flows. It is the heat that does it, that makes it warm and living at the source, and the further it flows the colder and more impure it gets. (p.180 Book 2)

I was asked the reason why virtuous folk who are in the good graces of God are so zealous to serve him. I said it was because they had tasted God and it were strange indeed if, once tasting and enjoying God, the soul could stomach aught beside. As the saint has it, once the soul tries God she finds the things that are not God repugnant and distasteful. (p.178)

He is Free and Strong

The devotee of justice is given up to justice, seized of justice, identified with justice. I once wrote in my book: The just man serves neither God nor creature: he is free; and the more he is just the more he is free and the more he is freedom itself. (p.204)

People who in a state of freedom and interior calm envisage God in peace and quiet and, when they are able to see him just as well in turmoil and disquiet, there is perfect equanimity . . . the lover of justice is possessed with justice and he is this virtue. (p.181)

The soul who is in truth translated into the Holy Trinity is immediately endowed by the Father's power and strength with the ability to do all things. (p.189)

Just indeed is he who lives in virtue and in virtuous deeds; who seeks not his own in anything, neither in God nor creature. That man dwells in God and God in him. (p.208)

That man is just (i.e. righteous) who is informed with and transformed into justice. The just lives in God and God in him, for God is born in the just and the just in God: at every virtue of the just God is born and is rejoiced, and not only every virtue but every action of the just wrought out of the virtue of the just and in justice; thereat God is glad, aye, thrilled with joy, there is nothing in his ground that does not dance for joy. To unenlightened people this is matter for belief but the illumined know.

The just seeks nothing in his work; only thralls and hirelings ask anything for work, or work for any why. If you would be informed with, transformed into righteousness, have no ulterior purpose in your work; form no idea in you in time or in eternity, not reward nor happiness nor this nor that, for truly such works are dead. (p.149)

Love Your Neighbour

Loving yourself you love all men as yourself. While you love anyone less than your own self you do not love yourself in truth; not till you love all men as yourself, all men in one man who is both God and man. The man who loves himself and all men as himself is righteous, absolutely just. (p.239)

When we talk of man we are talking of all creatures; Christ himself exhorted his disciples, "Go forth and preach the Gospel to all creatures", for creatures all culminate in man. Not but what, as being, God is pouring himself out into all creatures, to each as much as it can take. Which is a lesson to us to love all creatures equally with what we have received from God (though some are nearer to us by kinship or by natural friendship), as we are favoured equally with the boon of divine love. I sometimes seem to like one better than another, and yet I have the same good will towards that other person whom I have never seen, only, by asking more of me this one enables me to give myself more. God loves creatures all alike and fills them with his being. And we, too, should pour forth ourselves in love upon all creatures. (p.215)

There were once two doctors. One of them declared that the good man cannot be moved. The other disagreed. What I say is, the good man may forsooth be moved, but he cannot be changed for the worse. I know the good man is not easily hindered. (p.158)

The Just are Even-tempered

The just are they that take everything alike from God no matter what it is, big and little, good and bad, all the same, no more nor less, but one thing like another. (p.161)

*If You understand this You understand
all that Eckhart is saying*

The just are so set on justice that were God not just they would not care a fig for God; they are so staunch to right, so perfectly indifferent to self, they reck not of the pains of hell nor of the joys of heaven nor anything whatever. Were all the pangs of those in hell and all the pain borne or to bear on earth to be the fruits of justice, they would not mind one jot, so true they are to God and to right. To the just man nothing gives more pain, there is no greater hardship, than what is contrary to justice, equipoise. – How so? If one thing can cheer and another depress, you are not equable; to be cheerful one moment and less or not at all so, in the next uneven-tempered. But the devotee of right is so stable that what he loves is his very life, nothing can upset him, nor does he care for aught beside. St Augustine says, where the soul loves there she is, rather than where she gives life. – Our text sounds plain and commonplace enough, but there are few who realize the actual meaning of it. One who grasps the import of justice and the just will understand all I have to say. (p.161)

The Just Man does not have to be academically trained

By being free and unattached the unlettered man may in love and in longing receive wisdom and impart it. (p.176)

According to one master, many people arrive at specific understanding, at formal, notional knowledge, but there are few who get beyond the science and the theory; yet one man whose mind is free from notions and from forms is more dear to God than the hundred thousand who have the habit of discursive reason. God cannot enter in and do his work in them owing to the restlessness of their imagination. If they were free from pictures they could be caught and carried up beyond all rational concepts, as St Dionysius says, and also have the super-rational light of faith at its starting-point, where God finds his rest and peace to dwell and work in as he will and when he will and what he will. God is unhindered in his work in these so he can do in them his most precious work of all, working them up in faith into himself. These people no one can make out; their life is an enigma, and their ways, to all who do not live the same. To this truth and to this blessed life, to this high and perfect consummation no one can attain except in abstract knowledge and pure understanding. (p.334)

How to recognize the Just Man

Pious folks must have threefold discrimination. First, the understanding has to be sufficiently acute to give a clear and detailed view of the part that nature plays in whatever may befall them, so that they may realize it fully and discount it. Next, whatever they may have to do they must always see whether it is right in principle. Thirdly, their intelligence must be so subtle that they are able to discern, in the case of any inspiration or the very faintest light that is revealed to them, whether it comes from God or from some false spirit. (p.142 Book 2)

A good man is known by three things. One is singleness of will: all we call nature his will is free from. The second is clear understanding: any mental knowledge that she has his soul has fully mastered: she either approfounds it here or yonder in the common ground during illumination. The third is peace of mind: such images as may occur therein are no hindrance to the soul. (p.448)

The really perfect man is wont to be so dead to self, so lost in God to his own form, and so transformed in the will of God that his entire happiness consists, I swear, in knowing self and all for naught; in knowing God and God alone and, all unwitting of any will or choice except God's choice and will, in "knowing God", to quote St Paul, "even as he is known". God is doing all his knowing, doing all his willing, doing all his loving in himself. Our Lord says that eternal life is simply knowing. (p.52 Book 2)

Virtues

The great thing is, not to be content with virtues that are merely theoretical, obedience for example, and poverty, and so on; but we ourselves must practise the works and fruits of virtue, putting ourselves often to the test, and be willing and anxious to be called upon by people and made use of. And it is not enough to do the works of virtue, to obey, for instance, or be poor or give up things or in other ways humble and resign ourselves, but we must go further, never stopping till virtue in itself, in its cause, is won. And in proof that it is ours we shall find ourselves bent chiefly upon virtue and doing virtuous deeds spontaneously, with no idea of their being fine or important things – they are done as a matter of course and for love of virtue rather than any why. Then we have virtue in perfection, not before. (p.33 Book 2)

A heathen philosopher says that virtue, except for virtue's sake, is in no wise a virtue. If its object is praise or aught else, that is bartering virtue. ... The good man wants no praise, he wants to be praiseworthy. And our own doctors teach that virtue is so pure, so wholly abstract and detached from corporal things in the ground and summit of its nature that nothing whatever can occur therein without defiling virtue and introducing vice. Such is virtue by nature. (p.82)

He must not Dabble

Man must always do one thing, he cannot do them all. He must always be one thing and in that one find all. To try to do everything, this as well as that, to give up his own method for another which for the moment he likes better, believe me, is a fertile source of instability. (p.34 Book 2)

What one way has, what possibilities, with these God has furnished all good ways without exception, for one good never clashes with another, and by the same token people ought to realize they do wrong to say, when they come across or hear about some admirable person, that because he does not use their way it is all labour lost: they dislike his method, so they decry as well his virtues and intentions. That is wrong. We ought to pay far more respect to other people's methods and despise no one's way. But let each one stick to his own way and, bringing all other ways into line with that, profit in his own way by the merits of them all. Change of method makes for instability of mind as well as mode. What you get in one way may be got in any other provided it is sound and good and God is the only thing in view, nor are all men able to travel the same road. (p.23 Book 2)

A man should choose a good way and abide by it, embodying in it the good ways of all kinds, only taking care they are acceptable to God, not embarking upon one today and another tomorrow, then he need not be afraid of missing anything. With God we can miss nothing: God never misses anything, and in God's company, no more do we. (p.35 Book 2)

He must not Compete

What God is in the God-loving soul not a soul knows but the soul he is in. (p.134)

Happiness

Happiness comes from knowledge, from understanding the will of God and obeying. Anything other than this is a slow killing of oneself. It is the destruction of one's own nature. Happiness is an option open to us and we take it or not as we will.

Time and the things of time cause our distress, so when we reach beyond time we reach for God, to our own true nature, to happiness. God too is happy in our joy and all our fellow men are beloved, whatever the situation may be, either of good or of bad. We are not expected to "like" other people. Liking is changeable and superficial and it is self-rewarding. "I like him because he has qualities I enjoy", and so I am rewarded. Loving is deeper than individual quirks of personality. We love everybody by reaching down to our own nature, by finding the "eye of the hurricane" inside ourselves and knowing that the same essence lies, maybe hidden, in every other person. We are all children of God and it is in our nature to be happy.

God's love is not heavy, sombre, punitive, oppressive. God laughs with joy. The just man, the man who finds God, is relieved of care. He is free to laugh with God.

Happiness

Everyone desires happiness. As the philosopher has it: "All men desire to be." (p.81)

Happiness is Knowledge and Wisdom

The kernel of the prime conception and of eternal happiness is knowledge. (p.111)

Our happiness depends on our knowledge, our awareness of the sovran good which is God himself. I have one power in my soul fully sensible of God. I am as certain as I live that nothing is as close to me as God. God is nearer to me than I am to my own self; my life depends on God's being near to me, present in me. So he is also in a stone, a log of wood, only they do not know it. If the wood knew of God and realized his nearness like the highest angel does, then the log would be as blessed as the chief of all the angels. Man is more happy than a log of wood in that he knows and is aware of God, how near at hand God is. The better he knows it the happier he is, and the worse he knows it the more unhappy he is. He is not happy because of God's being in him and so near him or because of having God, but because he is aware of God, of his nearness to him; because he is God-knowing and God-loving, and such an one knows that God's kingdom is at hand. (p.171)

A philosopher once said: Real knowledge, even in this body, is intrinsically so delightful that the sum total of created things is nothing to the joys of pure perception. (p.171)

According to the philosophers, man's highest happiness consists in the mental exercise of wisdom. And the Father's whole delight, his perfect bliss, is this intellectual wont which is the birth of his Son. This birth he so enjoys that he puts his whole might into it and his entire nature. Accordingly, the soul having gotten the Son by a feat of understanding, in him possesses all that God can give, in one perfect joy and bliss. (p.131)

Happiness is Freedom from Time

Once gotten beyond time and temporalities we are free and joyous all the time; then is the fullness of time, then the Son of God is born in you. (p.227)

"Rejoice in God all the time", says St Paul. He rejoices all the time who rejoices above time and apart from time. (p.227)

Elsewhere I have declared, there is a power in the soul untouched by time and flesh, flowing from the Spirit, remaining in the Spirit, altogether spiritual. In this power is God, ever verdant, flowering in all the joy and glory of his actual self. Such dear delight, such inconceivable deep joy as none can fully tell, for in this power the eternal Father is procreating his eternal Son without a pause, the power being big with child, the Father's Son and its own self this self-same Son withal, in the unique power of the Father. Suppose a man absolute monarch, the sole possessor of all earthly goods; suppose he gave up all for God and was the poorest of the poor; and that God laid on him to boot a burden big as ever he did lay on mortal man, all which he bare down to his death and then God granted him one fleeting vision of his being in this power: so vehement would be his joy that poverty and suffering would be wiped out. Aye, though God gave him never any taste of heaven but this, yet would he have the guerdon of his passion, for God himself is in this power in the eternal *now*. If a man's spirit were always joined to God in this same power, he could not age. For the *now* wherein God made the first man and the *now* wherein the last man disappears and the *now* I speak in, all are the same in God where there is but *the now*. (pp.36-7)

Wherein does happiness lie most of all? Some masters say it lies in love. Others, it lies in knowledge and in love, and these come nearer the mark. We, again, contend it neither lies in knowledge nor in love, but there is in the soul one thing from which both knowledge and love flow and which itself does neither know nor love like the powers of the soul. Who knows this knows the seat of happiness. This has no before or after nor is it expecting anything to come, for it can neither gain nor lose. It is wanting, in the sense that it knows nothing about working in itself; but it just is itself, enjoying itself God-fashion. (p.219)

All our perfection, our whole happiness, depends on our traversing and transcending creature, time and state and entering the cause which is causeless. (p.434)

Happy the Man who listens to God

Happy the man who is busy attending to what God is saying in him. He is directly subject to the divine light ray. (p.83)

To have all that has being and is lustily to be desired and brings delight; to have it all at once and whole in the undivided soul and that in God, revealed in its perfection, in its flower, where it first burgeons forth in the ground of its existence, and all conceived where God is conceiving himself – that is happiness. (p.82)

Christ says: "If any will come after me, let him deny himself and take up his cross and follow me." That is: cast away care and let perpetual joy reign in your heart. Thus the child is born. And when the child is born in me, the sight of friends, of father, dead there before my eyes will leave my heart untouched. Were my heart moved thereby the child would not be born in me though peradventure its nativity is nigh. I maintain that God and his angels take such keen delight in every act a good man does that there is no joy like it. And accordingly, I say, the birth of this child in you brings you most keen delight in all good deeds done in this world, your joy being so continuous as to be never-ending. (p.34)

Now I maintain, if you turn from your own self and from created things, then in what measure you do this you attain to unity and happiness in your soul-spark; a thing which is immune from time and space. (p.153)

God's Happiness

He says, "His reward is with the Lord". He says WITH, meaning that the reward of the just is where God is himself; that the happiness of the just and God's happiness are one: the righteous are in bliss where God is in bliss. (p.153)

God enjoys himself. In the joy, wherein God enjoys himself he enjoys all creatures. (p.142)

He who loves only God in creatures and creatures in God only, that man finds real and true and equal comfort everywhere. (p.49 Book 2)

Loving our Brothers

He who loves God as he ought and must (whether he would or not) and as all creatures love him, will love his even-Christian as himself, rejoicing in his joys and hoping for his honour as much as for his own and treating the other like himself. By this means he is always happy whether in honour or in need, just as though he were in heaven and withal has more enjoyments than the blessings of himself alone. (pp.108-9)

It does indeed seem hard, as our Lord commands, to love our even-Christians as ourselves. The unenlightened say that we ought to love them just the same as they love themselves. Not so. We ought to love them no more than our own selves, which is not difficult. (pp.108-9)

Mark the fruits borne by a man when he is one with God: together with God he is bearing all creatures and big with beatitude for every creature in virtue of being one with him. (p.157)

The wise man says God has spread his nets and lines over all creatures and we can find and know him in any one of them if only we will look. (p.172)

God laughs and plays

The just lives in God and God in him, for God is born in the just and the just in God: at every virtue of the just God is born and is rejoiced, and not only every virtue but every action of the just wrought out of the virtue of the just and in justice; thereat God is glad, aye thrilled with joy, there is nothing in his ground that does not dance for joy. (p.149)

The soul will bring forth Person if God laughs into her and she laughs back to him. To speak in parable, the Father laughs into the Son and the Son laughs back to the Father; and this laughter breeds liking and liking breeds joy, and joy begets love, and love begets Person, and Person begets the Holy Ghost. (p.59)

Verily, verily, by God, by God and as God liveth, at the least good deed, the least good will, the least good desire, all the saints in heaven as well as the angels rejoice with such great joy as all the joys of this world cannot equal. With the saints, the higher the more joyful and all their joy combined is but a speck to the delight that God takes in this act. God plays and laughs in this good work, whereas all other works, those which redound not to God's glory, are dust and ashes in God's sight. Therefore he cries, "Ye heavens rejoice! God has comforted his people". (p.230)

Intuition of the Sovran Good, that is God! To have that is to have the life most worthy of any creature. God is willing his own clear conception and his own delight. What is willing in the Godhead? It is the Father watching the play of his own nature. What is this play? It is his eternal Son. There has always been this play going on in the Father-nature. Play and audience are the same. The Father's view of his own nature is his Son. The Father embraces his own nature in the quiet darkness of his eternal essence which is known to none except himself. The glance returned by his own nature is his eternal Son. So the Son embraces the Father in his nature for he is the same as his Father in his nature. Thus from the Father's embrace of his own nature there comes this eternal playing of the Son. This play was played eternally before all creatures. As it is written in the Book of Wisdom, "prior to creatures, in the eternal now, I have played before the Father in his eternal stillness". The Son has eternally been playing before the Father as the Father has before his Son. The playing of the two is the Holy Ghost in whom they both disport themselves and he disports himself in both. Sport and players are the same. (p.147)

The Unjust Man

It is the unjust man, Eckhart says, who is "stagnant, cold and insipid". He is the unattractive one, the bore, the one to avoid.

When asked who a seeker should go to for instruction he said, "One person who has mastered life is better than a thousand persons who have mastered only the contents of books. But no one can get anything out of life without God. If I were looking for a Master of learning I should go to Paris, to the colleges where higher studies are pursued but if I want to know about the depths of life, they could not tell me. Where then should I go?

"I should go then to someone who has a nature, an inner being, that is pure and free and nowhere else. There I should find the answer. People. Why do you search among the dead bones? Why don't you work for life eternal?"

The Unjust Man

How to recognize Him

The further off he [the unjust man] is from God the more stagnant and cold and insipid he will be. (p.180 Book 2)

The unjust man, whether he would or no, is the servant of illusion: serving the world and creature he is the bondman of sin. (p.204)

If the soul turns outwards towards external things she dies and God dies also in the soul. (p.201)

St Bernard says the most subtle temptation that can beset us is to occupy ourselves too much in outward works. (p.45)

Why

If we fail to see God that is due to our feeble desire no less than the concourse of creatures. Aim high, be high. (p.133)

Thou must be free from *not* . . . It is a question, what burns in hell? Doctors reply with one accord: self-will. But I maintain, *not* burns in hell. A simile! Suppose I take a burning coal and put it on my hand; then if I say the coal is burning me I do it great injustice. To define precisely what it is that burns me: *not* does; because the coal has in it something my hand has not. Observe, it is this very *not* that burns me. Did my hand contain what the coal is and can afford, it would possess the fire-nature altogether . . . Because God and those who are in sight of God have in them something pertaining to real happiness which those who are apart from God have not, therefore this *not* alone torments the souls in hell more than the personal will or any fire soever. (p.48)

No sinner can receive this light being full of sin and wickedness or darkness. As St John says, "The darkness neither receives nor comprehends the light." Because the avenues by which the light would enter are choked and obstructed with guile and darkness. Light and darkness are incompatible like God and creatures. Enter God, exit creatures. (pp.10-11)

No man was ever lost save for the reason that once having left his ground he has let himself become too permanently settled abroad. St Augustine says: Many there be that have sought light and truth but only abroad where they are not. They finally go out so far that they never get back nor find their way in again. Neither have these found the truth, for the truth is within in their ground, not without. (p.11)

Many good gifts received in maidenhood are not brought forth in wifely fruitfulness, reborn in praise and thanks to God. Such gifts corrupt and come to naught, man being no better and no happier for them. In this case his virginity is useless because to his virginity he does not add the perfect fruitfulness of wife. That is the mischief. (p.35).

However natural and proper God is to the mind once it turns aside to make common cause with creatures and falls into their ways, it becomes correspondingly enfeebled and less master of itself, a serious handicap to good intentions, which makes it barely possible to recover the lost ground. And even if he does so a man will always have to be on the defensive. (p.31 Book 2)

When the man in the soul, the intellect, is dead unchecked evil prevails. To separate soul and body is bad enough, but for the soul to be divorced from God, that is a far worse matter. (p.84)

Mistaking Virtue for the Truth

Though we meditate on the blessed works of our Lord's poverty and his humility yet, coveting them not ourselves, the thoughts are useless. And to covet them is useless too unless we diligently seek how we may acquire them.

We would fain be humble: but not despised. To be despised and rejected is the heritage of virtue. We would be poor too, but without privation. And doubtless we are patient except with hardships and disagreeables. And so with all the virtues. (pp.44-5)

Now consider who they were that sold and bought therein [in the Temple] and who they are still. Mark me well: I name none but the virtuous. Yet even so, I can point out who the merchants were, and still are to this day, that thus buy and sell: those whom our Lord drove forth and cast out. He still does so to those who buy and sell in this temple: he would not leave a single one therein. Lo, they are merchants all who, while avoiding mortal sin and wishing to be virtuous, do good works to the glory of God, fasts, for example, vigils, prayers, etc., all of them excellent, but do them with a view to God's giving them somewhat, doing to them somewhat, they wish for in return. All such are merchants. This is plain to see, for they reckon on giving one thing for another and so to barter with our Lord, though they are mistaken as to the bargain ... They be sorry fools who bargain with the Lord like this: they know little or nothing of the truth. God cast them out of the temple and drove them forth. For light and darkness cannot dwell together. (p.28)

Trying too hard. The Dangers of the Ego

A man should not dragoon himself: "Thou shalt do this at whatever cost." That would be wrong for so he lends importance to himself. If anything should chance to grieve or trouble or disquiet him, again he would be wrong for that means giving way to self. When, out of the depths of humiliation he calls on God for counsel and, bending low before him, accepts with quiet faith whatever he may send, then he is right. (p.141)

The devil talks virtue too, but he urges superfluous virtues: too much fasting and watching and kneeling, too much weeping, and his counsels are more in the nature of commands, as thus: "Do this or you are damned", or "are not good or perfect". An orgy of uncontrolled virtues with no definite aim, that is his cue, and the soul is afraid within her and gleans no satisfaction from his words. (p.447)

A poor man wills nothing. Some folks mistake the sense of this: those, for example, who win personal repute by penances and outward disciplines; and are highly esteemed, God a' mercy, though knowing so little of God's truth. To all outward appearances these men are holy, but they are fools within and ignorant of the divine reality. These men define a poor man as one who wills nothing, explaining this to mean that he never follows his own will at all but is bent on carrying out the will of God. In this they are not bad; their intention is good and we commend them for it; God keep them in his mercy. But I trow these are not poor men nor are they the least like them. They are much admired by those who know no better, but I say they are fools with no understanding of God's truth. (p.218)

Much prayer and fasting, strenuous work and so forth is the greatest folly if a man does not reform his ways but is irritable and restless. It behoves him to take stock, that man, of his morbid state and of all his faults, and turn his whole attention to overcoming them. (p.180 Book 2)

Deceiving Oneself

Some folks always want their own way; that is bad, that way lies sin. Those others are a trifle better who would like to do God's will and have no mind to go against it, yet when they are sick they wish God would choose to make them well. These people would have God, then, conforming to their will rather than they to his. (p.161)

It is lamentable how some people think themselves so far advanced, so one with God, although they have not yet abandoned self at all but hug themselves, like trivial things, in fortune and misfortune. They are precious far from what they think. They are full of notions and intentions. I sometimes say, if a man who seeks nothing finds nothing, what right has he to complain? After all he has found what he sought. To seek or purpose aught is to seek or purpose naught, and to pray for aught is to get naught. (p.229)

Foolish folk take bad for good and good for bad. (p.199)

Hell

Many a time I have laid it down that great workers, great fasters, great vigil keepers, if they fail to mend their wicked ways, wherein true progress lies, do cheat themselves and are the devil's laughing stock. (p.135)

Creatures without exception get their being from God, even the damned in hell persist on somewhat of his being.

Though they dwell not in God in felicity still they must go on without him, against their will, in damnation. (p.133)

Hell, torment really means the frequent lapsing of the soul from the purpose of God's effort, which is to bring the soul to life again. (p.199)

Theologians speak of hell. I will tell you what hell is. It is merely a state. Your state here is your eternal state. This is hell. Take an illustration. A thief who has incurred the penalty of death on being caught: picture his state of mind on seeing others happy! So do we feel and worse. And so with those in hell who see God and his friends: the height of torment, so the masters say. (p.317)

Sin

Inclination to sin is not sin, but consenting to sin, to give way to anger (for instance) is sin. (p.12 Book 2)

One to whom eternal light is given may well stoop to imperfection and sometimes fall an easier prey to frivolity and suchlike venial sins than another man.

"What is the cause of this propensity?"

It comes from being engrossed in one simple thing: multitudinous images disturb the soul, tossing her about with their various conceits. Once conceiving unity she is distracted by diversity. But as soon as she begins to see, it is as though it had never been and she can free herself completely without the slightest effort; which is a sign that she has eternal light. To see and be unable to escape would argue lack of eternal light. You know now how it is that people, even with eternal light, are prone to sin. St Paul sinned after he had been caught up. (p.454)

Forgiveness

I make bold to say that if you could suddenly and finally

set your face against all sin with real repugnance and distaste and resolutely turn to God, then, though you had committed every sin that ever was from the days of Adam, or that ever shall be done, the whole of it would be forgiven you outright and the pain as well, so that on dying then and there you would rise up before the face of God. (p.21 Book 2)

To have sinned is not sin once it is repented of. Let none consent to sin for anything in time or eternity, not mortal or venial or any sin whatever. He who is wise in the ways of God will not forget that his trusty and amiable God has brought him out of sin to a godly life, and of one who was a foe has made a friend, which is better than making a new earth. This is one of the best reasons why a man should range himself once for all upon the side of God, and it is astonishing how it fires a man with strong and lofty purpose and makes him give up all pretensions of his own. And once confirmed in the will of God no one would wish that there should not have happened the sin he fell into; not because it was ungodly but rather as committing you to greater love, who are abased and humbled by it, than as just a disobedience to God. Withal you can safely trust to God not to have sent it to you except to bring out your best side. Once a man is past all sinning, has turned his back on it for good and all, then God treats him as though he had never fallen into sin; he will not let his sins weigh for one moment with him. Though they were in number as the sins of all mankind God would never let them count but would be as friendly with him as he ever was with creature; if he finds him ready now he will take no notice of what he was before. God is a present God: as he finds you so he takes you and accepts you – not what you may have been but what you are this instant. All the wrong and reproach that is brought on God by sin he gladly bears and has borne many a year, in order that mortals might arrive at a lively understanding of his love and the more to rouse their love and gratitude and fan the flame of their devotion – the normal and proper reaction from their sin. For this reason God is willing to bear the brunt of sins and often winks at them, mostly sending them to people for whom he has provided some high destiny. See. Who was dearer to our Lord or more intimate with him than his apostles? Not one of them but fell into mortal sin, all of them were mortal sinners. In the Old Testament as well as in the New he repeatedly showed this to be true of those who afterwards were far the dearest to him; and still in our own day we rarely hear of anyone reaching a high level of perfection without some untowardness to start with, it being the purpose of our Lord that, recognizing his great mercy, we shall be spurred to more and truer devotion and humility. For with the renewal of rue love revives and waxes apace. (pp.18-19 Book 2)

The worse we think our sins to be the readier God is to forgive the sins, to come into the soul and drive them out, for everyone tries hardest to get rid of the things he dislikes, so the more and bigger the sins are the more pleased God is to pardon them, and the more prompt the more he hates them. When this divine repentance reaches up to God then, quicker than I can shut my eyes, all the sins have vanished in the sink of God, wiped out as utterly as though they had not been, by saving rue. (p.19 Book 2)

On no account let anyone suppose that he is far from God because of his infirmities or faults or for any other reason. If at any time your great shortcomings make an outcast of you and you cannot take yourself as being near God, take it then at any rate that he is near to you for it is most mischievous to set God at a distance. Man goes far away or near but God never goes far off; he is always standing close at hand, and even if he cannot stay he goes no further than the door. (p.23 Book 2)

God's Justice

Know that in itself God's justice is of a sternness that must make all tremble. Well knowing this, Christ said to his disciples: "Having done all that is possible to you, say, We are unprofitable servants." We learn this from St John also, who, though he did no sin to separate him from God yet likened himself to the beasts of the forest. Surely we know God's truth. I say moreover, God's justice is so harsh that, though a man do all the good works wrought by the company of saints now in eternal life, yet, being found in mortal sin (the first is pride; the second, slothfulness in any God's service; the third, hate; the fourth, anger; the fifth, greed; the sixth, overeating and drinking; the seventh, unchastity. These are the seven deadly sins) being found, I say, in one of these, he would be lost eternally. I hold it would avail him nothing for all the saints in heaven to intercede for him. I affirm, moreover, were Christ to supplicate his Father, and Mary his mother, it would not avail to save his soul. Further, concerning this I say that I would sooner have the man who sins a thousand mortal sins and knows it, than him who sins but one in ignorance; that man is lost. (p.316)

Touching the last day, people say, God shall judge. So he shall, but not as they think. Each man is his own judge in this sense: the state he then appears in he is in eternally. People frequently assert: The body shall rise with the soul. So it shall. But not as they think. The being of the body and the being of the soul go to form one being. Those souls who all their days have spent their time in God till God has come to be their being, to them God stays their being, body and soul eternally. Not so the wicked who have squandered their time on creatures, what their state is it continues to be, and this eternal lapsing from God and from his friends is called hell. Yet bear in mind that these same persons get their being from God or they would not be at all. So they are in God and God is in them. You see, they have the being of God. Take it like this. They are in God like a man with his life forfeit to some righteous Lord whose honour he has stolen and whose friends, and plotted frequently against his life; and now his Lord, who showed him only kindness in hopes of his reform, is vexed to find that he declines to mend. Holding him in the grip of justice, his Lord forbears to kill. He punishes the outrage on himself. First bound hand and foot, the man is cast into the lowest donjon among toads and reptiles and the foul water which is wont to lie in deepest dungeon keeps. Fetched up from there, he is disgraced before the world, that they may see his open shame and he their joy. So much the more his torment. Insult after insult do they heap upon him, shame unthinkable. . . . Even so it is permissible to say that man is at the court, for the donjon is the royal court as much as the hall is where the King stops with his friends: but conditions, you see, are different. Though not with that celestial race we spoke of. Know the grief endures eternally. I marvel that anyone who hears these words should dare to sin. Purgatory is so grievous in itself that anyone who knows the rights of it would stay no time in sin. (p.330)

Mark what sin is. It is born of negation. Negation's brood must be exterminated in the soul; while there is NOT in you you are not the Son of God. We weep and lament for want of something. The minus quantity must go, be cancelled out, if man is to become the Son of God and weep and wail no more. Man is not wood or stone: imperfection and naught. We shall not be like him until this minus is made good and we are all in all as God is all in all. (p.34)

4

Suffering. Images, Time, Unity

Suffering

Introduction

*I work in the academic Department of Surgery in a
London Teaching Hospital. I am nearing the end of a research project in which I teach control of pain to pre- and
post-operative patients having major surgery. Most of
what I know and teach about pain control comes from the
study of Eckhart.*

*Firstly, mind and body are one. "The soul is in the smal-
lest member as well as the body as a whole." When the
body suffers so does the mind. When the mind suffers so
does the body.*

*Secondly, pain and suffering are a necessary part of life.
Without the stimulus of pain we would learn nothing.
Those few unfortunate people born who can't feel pain
have difficulty even in surviving. Pain is a warning of
danger.*

*Thirdly, to conquer pain we must accept, not endure, it.
Acceptance and endurance are both physical as well as
mental states. Enduring something is waiting for it to end,
seeing it as something wrong which, eventually, must go
away, assuming that God has made a mistake and that
what is happening is not according to his will. The strength
to endure comes from looking forward to the time when
the pain is gone. In enduring – and the very word is derived
from "hardness" – the body is tense, which means that the
secretion of endorphins, the self-anaesthetizing substance*

the body secretes in response to pain, is inhibited. So it is like a vicious circle — pain, endurance, tension, pain2, endurance2, tension2 — pain3, endurance3, tension3. When Eckhart says "all suffering comes from loving, minding", it sounds as though he advocates stoicism, "endurance". He doesn't. In suggesting the alternative "not loving, not minding" he is talking about using the quality of detachment.

Was it not a proof of the true love Our Lady had for her Son, the "love beyond love", that she did not allow herself to be engulfed by her "loving and minding" of his suffering, that she was detached? That she didn't fall to pieces in front of him? Surely the greatest help she could give him was her demonstration of trust in the will of God which gave her the strength to survive. She then had strength to give to him.

Acceptance is a state of relaxation. Anyone who is relaxed is living in time-present. At any presentiment of the future or fear of the past acceptance of the present time is negated. Eckhart says "all suffering comes from loving, minding". It does. If "I still set store by the things of time", if I am unwilling to accept the will of God, whatever that may be, then I suffer because I am fighting God.

What Eckhart keeps on saying is that we have choice. If we suffer it is because we choose to do so (although if we do not know how to accept, to relax, we have got to learn). It is a possibility, in our nature, that we can so control pain and suffering, that we can have "peace in a life of pain".

Unless they ask me I don't talk to my patients about God. I teach them to accept, to relax, to concentrate, to focus their attention on the pain and to let go into it rather than using effort and will-power to fight against it. The moment they do this the pain, both of mind and body, is eased. But if they understand for themselves that what they are accepting is the "will of God" then, what they learn *about control of pain and suffering is a revelation for the rest of their lives.*

Suffering

A life of rest and peace in God is good; a life of pain in patience is still better; but to have peace in a life of pain is best of all. (p.172)

To the just man nothing gives more pain, there is no greater hardship, than what is contrary to justice, equipoise – how so? If one thing can cheer and another depress, you are not equable. . . . But the devotee of right is so stable that what he loves is his very life, nothing can upset him, nor does he care for aught beside. (p.161)

The swiftest steed to bear you to your goal is suffering; none shall ever taste eternal bliss but those who stand with Christ in depths of bitterness. Nothing is so gall-bitter as suffering, nothing so honey-sweet as to have suffered. (p.347)

The Cause of Suffering

All suffering comes from loving, minding: liking or minding is the alpha and omega of suffering. I trouble about temporal things because I mind about them, because I still set store by the things of time and do not yet love God wholeheartedly, with all the affection he demands and would make sure of getting. So is it to be wondered at if God is always sending us suffering and pain? (p.50 Book 2)

My Suffering may be of my own Choice

All sorrow comes from that whereof I am deprived by loss. If I mind the loss of outward things it is a certain sign that I am fond of outward things and really love sorrow and discomfort. Is it to be wondered at that I am unhappy when I

85

like discomfort and unhappiness; when my heart seeks and my mind gives to creature the good that is God's own? I turn towards creature, whence comes by nature all discomfort, and turn my back on that which is the natural source of happiness and comfort, so what wonder I am woebegone and wretched. The fact is, it is quite impossible for God or anyone to bring true solace to a man who looks for it in creatures. But he who loves only God in creatures and creatures in God only, that man finds real and true and equal comfort everywhere. (p.49)

What to do about it

When outward ills befall the good and righteous man then, if he keeps his even temper and his peace of mind, it is true, as I have said, that the righteous man is proof against external happenings. But if he is perturbed by these mishaps then it stands to reason that God is only just in sending trials to a person who, while pretending to be righteous and thinking himself so, is yet upset by so small a thing. (p.48 Book 2)

If you pour fresh water into a clean basin and all being clear and bright, stand it in a quiet place, then holding your face over it, you see it at the bottom as it really is. That is because the water is free from impurity and still. It is the same with people who, in a state of freedom and interior calm, envisage God in peace and quiet, and when they are able to see him just as well in turmoil and disquiet there is perfect equanimity: but if a man enjoys himself less in trouble and unrest, that augurs him not equable (unjust). (p.181)

Now you must know that people who resign themselves to God and diligently seek to do his will, to these, I say, whatever God may send will be the best. As God lives, be sure it is the very best, and there can be no better way. Some other may seem better yet is not so good for you; God wills this way and not that, therefore this way is bound to be the best. Sickness or poverty, hunger or thirst, what God does give you or what he does not, that is the very best for you, aye, though it be fervour or the interior life which, alas, you lack. Whatever you have or have not, accept it all to the glory of God, and then whatever he sends for you will be for the best.

Perhaps you will say, "How can I tell whether it is God's will or not?" If it were not God's will it would not be. Neither sickness nor anything else happens to you without God's will. And so, knowing it to be God's will you ought to rejoice in it and to be so content with it that any pain shall lose its sting for you: aye, even in extremity of pain to feel the least affliction or distress were altogether wrong: accept it from God as the best since it is bound to be the best thing for you. (p.107)

Again, turn everything to good account, means, love God the same in poverty as wealth, hold him as dear in sickness as in health. The heavier to bear the lighter to bear; like two buckets, the heavier the one the lighter the other, and so the more one gets rid the easier the riddance. The God-lover parts with the world as cheerfully as with an egg. The more he gives up the easier it grows. (p.165)

Seneca, the heathen philosopher, inquires, What is the greatest comfort in suffering and discomfort? To take it all, he says, as though it had been wished and prayed for. Having wished and prayed that God's will be done then if it is you have no cause to groan. It was a pagan master who exclaimed, "Lord, supreme Father, sole ruler of the highest heaven, all that thou wilt I am prepared for, vouchsafe me will and that will in accordance with thine own." (p.52 Book 2)

"If any man will come after me" etc . . . That is: cast away care, let perpetual joy reign in your heart. Thus the child is born. And when the child is born in me, the sight of friends, of father, dead there before my eyes, will leave my heart untouched. (p.34)

Would you know for certain whether your sufferings are yours or God's? Tell by these tokens. Suffering for yourself, in whatever way, the suffering hurts you and is hard to bear. But suffering for God and God alone your suffering does not hurt you, nor does it burden you, for God bears the load. Believe me, if there were a man willing to suffer on account of God and of God alone, then though he fell a sudden prey to the collective sufferings of all the world it would not trouble him nor bow him down, for God would be the bearer of his burden. If the burden they put upon my neck is forthwith shouldered by another I would as lief a hundred pounds as one, for not to me is it heavy or distressful. In brief: man's sufferings for God and God alone he makes both light and pleasant. (p.37)

Folks tell us of the holy life, how they have suffered. To tell the tale of what our Lord's friends suffered time would be all too short. I say: they did not suffer. The least suspicion of God-consciousness and sufferings would be all forgotten. This may well happen while the soul is in the body. I say more: while yet in the body a soul may reach oblivion of its travail not to remember it again. Further I hold: to him who suffers not for love, to suffer is suffering and is hard to bear. But he who suffers for love does not suffer, and this suffering is fruitful in God's sight. It follows, friends, that by contriving to die in God gladly, we go scot-free from suffering. (p.323)

We ought really to leave all suffering to the body with its lower powers and senses, while the spirit ascends with entire power and plunges, free, into its God. The sufferings of the senses and the lower powers do not trouble it, neither does their strife, for the longer and harder fought the battle the finer and more glorious the triumph and the fruits of victory. (p.29 Book 2)

In God there is no sorrow or suffering or distress. And, if you would be free from all adversity and pain, turn and cleave to God and to God only. Doubtless all your ills are due to your not turning to God and to God alone. (p.47 Book 2)

What not to do

People have a way of saying, when it falls to them to do or suffer something, "If only I knew it was the will of God I would gladly suffer and put up with it". Dear God! What a question for a sick man to ask, Does God intend me to be ill? He ought to know it is the will of God by the very fact of being ill. (p.140)

It is a certain sign of God's not being in his heart, but only mortal, temporal creature when anyone turns outwards in search of consolation. (p.51 Book 2)

Judge then for yourselves of your love! If you do indeed love God you will like nothing better than that which best enables him to work his will in us. However great may seem the pain or the privation, unless you take delight in it as great as in your ease and plenty, it is wrong. (pp.107-8)

There are two births of man; one in the world, the other one out of the world and ghostly, in God. Would you know if your child is born and if he is naked? . . . If your heart is heavy, except for sin, your child is not born. In your anguish you are not yet mother; you are in labour and your hour is near. . . . The birth is not over till your heart is free from care; then man has the essence and nature and substance and wisdom and joy and all that God has. (p.34)

God's Comfort

No hardship or discomfort is without some comfort, no loss without some gain, and that is why St Paul declares that God's good faith and his natural kindness would not permit of any suffering or trial being unsupportable, more than one could bear. He always provides some consolation for the help of man. Withal the saints and doctors teach that God and nature cannot brook the being or existence of undiluted evil. (p.49 Book 2)

A man, once he escapes for good from his possessions, is fenced about with God, and creature cannot touch him without first encountering God, and anything to reach him must go by way of God so it gets a flavour of him and becomes divine. However great the suffering if it comes through God God bears the brunt of it. Not the least suffering can befall a man, but so far as he shifts it onto God – some mischance it may be, or unpleasantness – it falls infinitely harder upon God than on the man and is more against the grain with him than with anyone. (p.17 Book 2)

The fount and living artery of universal good, essential truth and perfect consolation is God, God only, and everything not God has in itself a natural bitterness, discomfort and unhappiness and does not make for good, which is of God and is the same as God, but lessens, dims, and hides the sweetness, joy and comfort that God gives. (pp.48-9 Book 2)

Our Lord said to his disciples, "It is expedient for you that I should go away, for while I am with you the Holy Ghost will not come unto you". With these words our Lord comforted his disciples after supper on the eve of his departure, knowing full well that they were sorrowful at finding he was going to leave them. Our Lord will not long suffer his lovers to be troubled. (p.191)

Images

God scorns to work among Images

God works without instrument and without image. And the freer you are from images the more receptive you are to his interior operation. (p.7)

"God has no image nor likeness of himself seeing that

he is intrinsically all good, truth and being." (p.7)

The smallest of creaturely images that takes shape in you is as big as God. . . . How so?

It shuts out the whole of God. As soon as this image appears God disappears with all his Godhood. As this image fades out God comes in. No temporal image is so Godly but three times harms the soul first, it vexes spirituality; next, it tarnishes her purity; and thirdly it disturbs detachment.

. . . What does God do to my mind?

. . . Transcends yourself and represses creatures: God does that to your mind.

Now you must know that inwardly the soul is free from means and images, that is why God can freely unite with her without form or similitude. (p.5)

There is the question whether the soul brings forth the eternal Word in images or imageless? Remember this. When the soul resigns herself to God and is atoned with him and God undertakes her work, she is receptive merely and leaves God to act. Here the soul is pregnant without form or image, for anything conceived in form or image trenches upon time and place and is akin to creatures; whence it follows the more the work is of the soul the less it is of God. The soul conceives more truly without images than in them, for this birth is more by way of Godhood than of selfhood. But we may still enquire, in which image does the soul best succeed in giving birth to the eternal Word? There are three kinds of images. The first the soul takes in from without through the senses. The second the soul conjures up from within by thinking on the childhood of our Lord or on his martyrdom; but all images so gotten are called divine births in the soul. The third kind of images is given to the soul by God direct. It is in these last that the soul conceives the best. (p.38)

According to one master, many people arrive at specific understanding, at formal, notional, knowledge, but there are few who get beyond the science and the theory; yet one man whose mind is free from notions and from forms is more dear to God than the hundred thousand who have the habit of discursive reason. God cannot enter in and do his work in them owing to the restlessness of their imagination. If they were free from pictures they could be caught and carried up beyond all rational concepts, as St Dionysius says, and also have the super-rational light of faith as its starting-point, where God finds his rest and peace to dwell and work in as he will and when he will and what he will. (p.334)

An image has two properties. First, it receives its being from the thing whose image it is, immediately and above will, for it is a natural product, sprouting out of its nature as a branch does out of a tree. Any face thrown on a mirror is, willy-nilly, imaged theron. But its nature does not appear in its looking-glass image: only the mouth, nose and eyes, just the three features, are seen in the mirror. God reserves it to himself to display in his reflections, at once his nature, all he is, and all he can, and this above his will. His image is prior to his will, will following the image, for out of his nature there leaps first his image, focusing into itself the whole promise of his nature and his essence, all his nature pouring out into his image the while it abides intact within itself. Now the masters locate this image not in the Holy Ghost but in the middle Person, for the Son, being the earliest issue of his nature, is therefore called his Father's express image, and not the Holy Ghost. (p.51)

Reality is not an Image

God needs no image and has no image: without image, likeness or means does God work in the soul, aye, in her ground whereinto no image did ever get but only himself with his own essence. This no creature can do. (p.5)

Were any image present there would not be real union and in real union lies your whole beatitude. (p.6)

An image is not itself, neither is it its own. So an image received into the eye is not the eye itself nor has it any real existence in the eye but is merely suspended from and tethered to the thing it is the image of, whereto it entirely belongs and wherefrom it gets its being and is being that same being. Note well my definition of an image. There are four points to bear in mind and haply others will occur to you. An image is not itself, neither is it its own: it is solely that thing's whose reflection it is, and it is due to this alone that it exists at all. Things apart from the thing whose image it is, it is not and does not belong to. The image takes its being direct from the thing whose image it is, having one nature therewith and being the very same being. This is not a subject for discussion in the schools, though one may well propound it from the professorial chair.

You are always asking how you ought to live. Lay then to heart this answer: Just as the image is here said to do, even so it behoves you to live. Be his and belonging to him, not your own and belonging to yourself nor withal to anyone. (p.52)

When the soul-powers contact a creature they set to make of the creature an image and likeness which they absorb. By it they know the creature. Creatures cannot go into the soul, nor can the soul know anything about a creature which she has not willingly taken the image of into herself. She approaches creatures through their present image; an image being a thing that the soul creates with her powers. Be it a stone, a rose, a man, or anything else that she wants to know about, she gets out the image of it which she has already taken in and is thus able to unite herself with it. But an image received in this way must of necessity enter from without through the senses, consequently there is nothing so unknown to the soul as herself. (p.5)

Time

Getting beyond time is not so uncommon. It's a matter of intensity, the river of consciousness running deeply, not dispersed shallowly over a wide course. We often say "Time stood still" and always it is in response to some intense experience.

Looking forwards and backwards is how we lose joy, how we become fragmented, shallow and diversified.

Time is a division and while we are divided in time we cannot be at one with God. Out of time there can be no boredom, no anxiety, no depression, for in such states we see time as a replication and there is no such thing. Remember this may be when you say the Our Father for the millionth time, or when you wake up in the morning feeling pain or suffering. Each day, each moment of time, is unique and has unlimited possibilities. We have the choice to become trapped in time or not.

Time

The Fullness of Time

Once gotten beyond time and temporalities we are free and joyous all the time; then is the fullness of time, then the Son of God is born in you. (p.227)

Time is fulfilled when time is done. He who in time has his heart established in eternity and in whom all temporal things are dead, in him is the fullness of time. (p.227)

If someone had the knowledge and the power to gather up the time and all the happenings of these six thousand years, and all that is to come before the world ends to boot, all this, summed up into one present now, would be the fullness of time. (p.81)

When time drops from you your time is fulfilled. Again

time is fulfilled when it is finished, that is in eternity. Time ends when there is no before and after: when all that is is here and now, and you see at a glance all that has ever happened and shall ever happen. Here there is no before or after; everything is present, and in this immediate vision I possess all things. (p.236)

St Paul says: "In the fullness of time God sent his Son." St Augustine was asked what it meant, this fullness of time. It is the fullness (or end) of the day when the day is done: then the day is over. Certain it is that there is no time where this birth befalls, for nothing hinders this birth so much as time and creature. It is an obvious fact that time affects neither God nor the soul. Did time touch the soul she would not be soul. If God were affected by time he would not be God. Further, if time could touch the soul, then God could not be born in her. The soul wherein God is born must have escaped from time, and time must have dropped away from her; she must be absolutely one in will and desire. (pp.80-1)

The Malady of Time. And Number

If I could see God with my eyes the same as I see colours, that would not be right for that which is visible is temporal. The temporal taken according to time is taken at its lowest value. *Now* is time and place in itself. While man has time and place, number and quantity, he is not as he should be, is not just and God is remote and not his own. (p.209)

An ancient philosopher says the soul is made in between one and two. The one is eternity, ever alone and without variation. The two is time, changing and given to multiplication. He means to convey that the soul in her higher powers touches eternity, God to wit, while her lower powers being in contact with time make her subject to change and biased towards bodily things, which degrade her. (p.134)

Nothing hinders the soul from knowing God so much as

time and place. Time and place are fractions, God is an integer. So if the soul knows God at all she must know him above time and space, for God is neither this nor that as these manifold things are: God is one. (p.172)

This spirit knows no time or number: number does not exist except for the malady of time. Other root has it none save in eternity, where there is no number except one, this spirit, transcending number, breaks through into multiplicity and is transfixed by God, and by the fact of his piercing me I pierce him in return: God leads this spirit into the desert, into the solitude of its own self, where it is simply one and is welling up in itself. This spirit has no why, for if it had a why the unity would also have its why. This spirit is in unity and freedom.

What we know we must know in its cause. We never really know anything in itself till we know it in its cause. There is no understanding it until we apprehend it in its origin. Just as life is never perfected till it returns to its original source, wherein life is real being. The thing that keeps us from remaining there is, as the philosopher explains, our being in contact with time. What time can touch is temporal and mortal. The philosopher states that heavenly progression is eternal. True, it gives rise to time, and that makes it mortal. In its course it is eternal, all unwitting of time, in other words, the soul obeys the laws of abstract being. (p.207)

Aliquando, to those who are instructed, is the same as *when* and expresses time, which is what keeps the light from reaching us. There is no greater obstacle to God than time. He means not time alone but temporalities; not only temporal things but temporal affections; not only temporal affections but the very taint and aroma of time; for as where an apple has lain the smell lingers, so with the contact of time. According to our best authorities the visible heavens and the sun and the stars have nothing to do with time except bare contact with it. This I cite as showing that the soul, which towers high above the heavens, has, at her very summit, no connection with time at all. (p.237)

If God gave himself to the soul here in time she would be vexed. So he gives her himself in eternity, in the perennial now, up-springing freshly without ceasing. (p.77)

The Now and the Newness of Time

The masters ask, "Has the Son been born?" We say: "No." The masters ask, "Is the Son going to be born?" We say, "No."

The masters are answered: "The Son is fully born." He is being born anew, unceasingly. (p.76)

In her actuality she [the soul] is, like the Father, making all things new. (p.85)

We shall be like the angels. Perception here means seeing in the light that is in time, for anything I think of I think of in the light that is in time and temporal. But angels perceive in the light that is beyond time and eternal. They know in the eternal now. Men know in the now of time. The now of time is infinitely short but, take away this now of time, and you are everywhere and have the whole of time. (p.127)

Again he says, "a little and ye shall not see me." While time and world, which is little, is within you, you shall not see me. The angel swore on his eternal life that when this life is done there shall be no more time. And in his gospel St John quite plainly states, "the world was made by him and they knew him not." In fine then, to quote a heathen doctor, world-and-time is a little thing. It is out of world-and-time that we see God. (p.111)

First it [the intellect of the soul] is detached from here and now. Here and now, that, in other words, is time and place. *Now* is the minimum of time; not a fragment of time nor a fraction of time: a smack, a connection, an end of time. Small though it be it must go; everything

97

time touches has to go. (p.115)

He who would worship the Father must take himself into eternity in his desires and hopes. There is one, the loftiest part of the soul, which stands above time and knows nothing of time or of body. The happenings of a thousand years ago, days spent millenniums since, are in eternity no further off than this moment I am passing now; the day to come a thousand years ahead or in as many years as you can count, is no more distant in eternity than this very instant I am in. (pp.41-2)

Our doctors teach that in God there is no yesterday nor morrow, it is today and now all the time in God. (p.129)

In eternity, exalted above time, man does one work with God. People sometimes ask how man can do the work that God was doing a thousand years ago and in a thousand years will be doing still. They cannot understand it. But in eternity is no before or after; the happenings of the past millennium and the future one and now, in eternity are all the same. God's doings of a thousand years ago and now and a thousand years to come are but one single act. It follows that the man who is exalted above time into eternity will do with God what he did in the past and also what he does in the next thousand years. This is a matter of knowledge to the wise and belief to fools. (p.150)

Again I take a span of time, which need not be today or yesterday. But if I take the now that includes all time. The now wherein God made the world is as near this time as the now I am speaking in this moment, and the last day is as near this now as was yesterday. (pp.210-11)

The soul's day and God's day are different. In her natural day the soul knows all things above time and place; nothing is far or near. And that is why I say, this day all things are of equal rank. To talk about the world as being made by God tomorrow, yesterday, would be talking nonsense. God makes the world and all things in this present now. Time gone a thousand years ago is now as present and as near to God as this very instant. (p.209)

This power [of the soul] has naught in common with naught, it knows no yesterday or day before, no morrow or day after (for in eternity there is no yesterday or morrow): therein it is the present now; the happenings of a thousand years ago, a thousand years to come, are there in the present and the antipodes the same as here. (p.228)

Blessed, supremely blessed, are they who are installed in the eternal now, transcending time and place and form and matter, unmoved by weal and woe or wealth or want, for in so far as things are motionless they are like eternity.

The heaven adjoining the eternal now, wherein the angels are, is motionless, immovable. But the heaven next to that which touches the eternal now, wherein the Angels are, and between (that and) the heaven where the sun is, is set in motion by angelic force, revolving once in every hundred years. The heaven the sun is in, moved by angelic force, goes round once a year. The heaven the moon is in, again, is driven by angelic force and goes round once a month. The nearer the eternal now the more immovable they are, and the further off and more unlike to the eternal now the easier to move. The heaven of the sun and moon and stars is moved by the impulse of their angel, so that they are spinning in this temporal now; and the eternal now imparts their motion, that being so energetic that from the motion the eternal now imparts, all things derive their life and being. Now the lowest powers of the soul are nobler than the highest part of heaven, where it adjoins the angels and the eternal now. Moreover, all things get their life and being from the motion there imparted by the eternal now; and if that is so noble, then what would you expect where the soul in her superior powers contacts the ground of God? How exalted, think you, that must be? Follow then after this now, and reach this now and possess this eternal now. May we stand next to the eternal now and so be in possession of it. (p.56)

This light [of grace] is vastly potent, not merely being in itself exempt from time and place, but anything it falls upon it robs of time and place and bodily semblance and everything extraneous thereto. As I have often said before, were there no time nor place nor aught beside it would all be one being. The man who is in this sense one and casts himself into the ground of humility, there will be watered with grace. (p.66)

Now enough of those who have no object in eternity, but one thing more of those who are objectless in time. What is meant by object? There are two objects: one is otherness (not I); the other is a man's own proper self (his I).

The first otherness is *becoming*, all that has come into existence; such things breed otherness and pass away. This applies to the passage of time.

He who knows one matter in all things remains unmoved. For matter is the subject of form and there can be no matter without form nor form devoid of matter. Form without matter is nothing at all; but matter ever cleaves to form and is one undivided whole in every single part of it. Now since form in itself is naught, therefore it moves nothing. And since matter is perfectly impartible, therefore it is unmoved. This man then is unmoved by form or matter and is therefore objectless in time. (p.123)

For the *now* wherein God made the first man, and the *now* wherein the last man disappears, and the *now* I speak in, all are the same in God where there is but *the now*. (p.37)

Unity

Union with God

The best work that we can do is to prepare for union with the present God and wait for this with fixed intention. (p.45)

The exalted spark wherein we see the light divine, that never parts from God nor is there anything between. (p.59)

Those who are steadfast in the face of multiplicity, behold what light and grace are revealed to them. (p.147)

God says, "I am the first and the last". No difference exists either in the nature of God or in the Persons so far as they are one in nature. The divine nature is one and each of the Persons also is one, the same one as their nature. Distinction in being and existence is taken as *same* and is one. Where it is not in [God] it takes on and has and shows difference. In one God is found, so to find God a man must be one. Our Lord says: "A man went out". In difference (separation) we find neither one nor reality, nor God nor rest nor bliss nor satisfaction. Be one, that you may find God! And truly, if you were really one you would stay one in separation, and separation would be one to you, so nothing could stand in your way. One remains equal to one in a thousand thousand stones just as much as it does in four stones, and a million is a simple number just as much as four. (p.83 Book 2)

While there is more and less in you God cannot dwell nor work in you. These things must go out for God to come in; except you have them in a higher, better way: multitude summed up to one in you. Then the more of multiplicity the more there is of unity for the one is changed into the other. (p.227)

What are we to understand by God? That he is the one power. Let us therefore unify ourselves so that this one power may energize in us. (p.147)

It is not enough, in seeking union with God, to enjoy occasional detachment of the mind, it needs expert, habitual detachment, going on before and after; then we receive great things from God and God in these things. (p.32 Book 2)

101

Where they find God there they find the soul, and where the soul there God. Never was such close union; the soul is much more closely knit to God than body is to soul in the making of a man. The union is more intimate than when a drop of water is poured into a vat of wine; that would be wine and water, but the other is transformed into the same so that no creature can detect a difference. (p.28 Book 2)

The angel was sent to the soul to bring her back to the very same form wherein he is formed, for knowledge comes by likeness. The soul is capable of knowing all things and she never rests till she attains her original form wherein all things are one. (p.75)

Theologians teach that the angel hosts are countless, the number of them cannot be conceived. But to one who sees distinctions apart from multiplicity and number, to him I say, a hundred is as one. Were there a hundred Persons in the Godhead he would still perceive them as one God. (p.81)

Remember. If you love right as God you do not love right as right, therefore you neither take it nor love it as a whole but as divided. (p.124)

Beyond Diversity

The more a thing participates in a common nature, the more it is one with the impartibility of the common nature, the more impartible it is itself. To the whole truth God help us. (p.125)

Birth is tantamount to becoming. In the eternal birth is her becoming; there she becomes so wholly one that she has no other being than the self-same being which is his, to wit, the being of the soul. This being is the source of all works wrought by God in heaven and earth. It is the ground and origin of all divine activity. In dying to her own nature and her being and her life the soul is born in her divinity. That is her becoming. She becomes so wholly one that there is no distinction except that he stays God and she stays soul. (p.186 Book 2)

Why did he [God] say no more than one word? Because all things are present in his mind. If I could grasp in one idea all the thoughts I ever had or ever shall have, then I should have one word, no more, for the mouth utters what is in the heart. (p.186 Book 2)

If the soul is to be simple she must withdraw from multiplicity into his one conception. That can happen here only now and then. (p.148)

According to St Dionysius, burial in God is nothing but the crossing over into uncreated life. This crossing is beyond the ken of multitudinous knowledge. (p.195)

There is something transcending the soul's created nature, not accessible to creature, non-existent; no angel has gotten it, for his is a clear (intelligible) nature, and clear and overt things have no concern with this. It is akin to Deity, intrinsically one, having naught in common with naught. Many a priest finds it a baffling thing. It is one; rather unnamed than named, rather unknown than known. (pp.204-5)

I used to wonder (it is many years ago) whether I should be asked why one blade of grass is so unlike another; and as it happened I was asked why they are so different. I said, it is more marvellous they are so much alike. One philosopher says that the blades of grass are all different owing to the superfluity of the goodness of God which he pours out abundantly into all creatures the more to show his majesty. I said it is more wonderful that the blades are alike, explaining that just as all the angels are the same in their original pure nature so all the grasses are the same and all things are identical. (p.223)

God and the soul are so entirely one that God has not a single thing to tell him from the soul, nor is he any other than the soul. (p.127)

God is inseparate from things; he is more innate in them than they are in themselves. And man should be inseparate from things: not as cleaving to self but as wholly detached from himself; thus he is inseparate from all things and he is in all things. (p.128)

Now our doctors say: Natural acts make for unity. God vouchsafes himself, gives himself, as a whole to the soul in order she may be one with him. (p.132)

As St James says, "Every good gift and every perfect gift come down from above from the Father of lights." We may deduce from this that all things are one light radiated by the Father for the purpose of revealing his own hidden light. And as all things have been one light proceeding forth, so also they are all one light which is flowing back, if they turn not away therefrom of their own free will. (p.147)

Hindrances to Union

There are three hindrances to union of the soul with God. First, her being too much divided, not simple (pure) enough. The soul is not simple in her relations with creatures. The second one is attachment to temporal things. And thirdly, being fond of the body will prevent union with God.

Also there are in the soul three aids to union with God. First, the soul being one and undivided: to be atoned with God she has to be as pure as God is. Next, her being above herself and all temporal things and keeping hold of God. Thirdly, detachment from all mortal things and perfect freedom of action. (p.189 Book 2)

Three things prevent a man from knowing God at all. The first is time, the second body, and the third is multiplicity or number. (p.227)

5

The Weapons We Have

Wisdom

We can all be Wise. We can teach Wisdom

The wise man says, God has spread his nets and lives all over creatures, and we can find and know him in any one of them if only we will look. (p.172 Book 1)

By being free and unattached the unlettered man may in love and longing receive wisdom and impart it (p.176)

Jesus reveals himself in the soul in infinite wisdom, himself to wit, the wisdom wherein the father knows himself in full paternal power. The very Word, which is wisdom itself, and all that is therein, is, at the same time ONE ALONE. When wisdom is in union with the soul, doubt, error and illusion are entirely removed, she is set in the bright pure light of God himself, as says the prophet, "Lord in thy light shall we see light." Then God is known by God in the soul; she discerns with his wisdom both herself and all things. She knows not this same wisdom with herself, but with this wisdom she discerns the Father fruitful in travail and his real being in impartible oneness void of all distinctions. (p.31)

One who is minded to attain this wisdom will need humility and industry and a penetrating passivity. (p.174 Book 2)

Doctors declare that the wisdom we learn here stays with us yonder. St Paul says it will go. A philosopher once said, "Real knowledge, even in this body, is intrinsically so delightful that the sum total of created things is nothing to the joys of pure perception." Yet noble though it may be, it is but contingent; as one small word to all the world even thus insignificant is all the wisdom we learn here compared with the whole and perfect truth. (p.75)

Wisdom and Goodness

Wisdom and goodness are the same in God. What wisdom is that very same is goodness and the rest. If in him wisdom were one thing and goodness were another there would be no satisfaction for the soul in God, but the soul has a natural inclination to God, and creatures all have an innate longing for wisdom. Take a soul overflowing with goodness, if goodness were one thing and wisdom another that soul would with pain have to give up her goodness if she wanted to pour forth in wisdom. (p.187 Book 2)

Goodness

He who has once been touched by truth, by right, by good, though it entailed the pangs of hell, that man could never turn therefrom, not for an instant (p.42)

Essence is self absorbed: not an effusion but an inner fusion. And unity is one and self-contained: aloof from everything and free from outside intercourse. But goodness is the melting and running out of God, his diffusion to the whole of creatures. Essence is the Father, Unity the Son, and goodness is the Holy Ghost. (p.99)

Goodness is a garment under which God is concealed, and will takes God in this garment of goodness. If God had no goodness my will would repudiate God. It would be unseemly to robe a king in drab on his coronation day. I am not happy by reason of God's goodness. Never should I think of asking God to beatify me with his goodness, for he could not do it. Goodness is his vesture. (p.213)

Perception

Perception here means seeing in the light that is in time and temporal, for anything I think of I think of in the light that is in time and temporal. But angels perceive in the light that is beyond time and eternal. (p.127)

Perception leads the way. It is the princess seeking the prince upon the mountain top, in virgin realms; she proclaims him to the soul, and the soul to nature, and nature to the passions of the body. (p.75)

Truth

A philosopher says: "He who has once been touched by truth, by right, by good, though it entailed the pangs of hell, that man could never turn therefrom not for an instant." (p.42)

The Son alone is the truth and not the Father, save in the sense that they are one truth in their essence. That is truth which reveals what I have in my heart without likeness. This revelation is truth. The Son alone is the truth. The whole content of the Father's love he speaks at once in his Son. This utterance, this act, is the truth. (p.78)

Try diligently, therefore, to get some grasp of truth: in the conception of it your own wont is altogether lost and you live in truth. Those exalted ones who stand therein can never be disjoined from God. They are the blessed who know God is himself eternally. (p.149)

Whoso is unable to follow this discourse let him never mind. While he is not like this truth he shall not see my argument, for it is the naked truth straight from the heart of God. May we so live as to experience it eternally. (p.221)

Knowledge

The kernel of the prime conception and of eternal happiness is knowledge. (p.111)

"Cephas" means a head. Understanding is the head of the soul. The superficial notion is that love stands first. But the soundest arguments expressly state (what is the truth) that the kernel of eternal life lies rather in knowledge than in love. (p.83)

Knowledge is the flux, for knowledge is hotter than love. But two are better than one. And this knowledge is laden with love. Love is fooled and caught by kindness: in love I hang about the gate turning a blind eye to the authentic vision. Even stones have love, a love that seeks the ground. If I insist on goodness in the first effusion and seize this at the point where it is good, then I shall seize the gate, not God himself. Knowledge is the better as being the head and front of love. Love is the will to, the intention. No single thought attaches to this knowledge: wholly detached and self-forsaken it runs all bare into the arms of God and grasps him in himself. (p.96)

Whatever else one may know one does not know God. (p.106)

If an angel sees another angel or anything God has made, he does so by some means. But himself and God he sees immediately. If my soul knows an angel she knows him by some means and in an image, an image imageless, not in an image such as they are here. Soul and angel are material things compared with God. Angelic knowledge, anything created, is a means. Which God wholly lacks: he is known without means, without little. For my soul to know God with nothing between thou must be with me and I with thee. (p.112)

St Paul tells us, "We shall know God as we are known". As God knows himself so shall we know him; as he sees all things in himself so shall we see all things in him. "We shall know as we are known", St Paul says. The little being cleared away, I shall see as I am seen, as he sees himself, without little, with nothing between; all in himself and in him all things, nothing outside him: and we too shall know without little and without means. (p.112)

Self-Knowledge

"Know thyself, that is the way to God." (p.202 Book 2)

St Augustine teaches about three kinds of knowledge. The first is bodily knowledge; the eye, for instance, is sensible of images. The second is mental but still admits of images of bodily things. The third is in the interior mind, which knows without image or likeness, and this knowledge is like unto the angels. (p.243)

Pious folk must have threefold discrimination. First, the understanding has to be sufficiently acute to give a clear and detailed view of the part that nature plays in whatever befalls them, so that they may realize it fully and discount it. Next, whatever they may have to do they must always see whether it is right in principle. Thirdly, their intelligence must be so subtle that they are able to discern, in the case of any inspiration or the very faintest light that is revealed to them, whether it comes from God or from some false spirit. (p.142 Book 2)

The willing poor, unsolaced by corruptibles, descend into the valley of humility. They are pursued by insult and adversity, the best school of self-knowledge. And self-knowledge gets God-knowledge. (p.45)

Three things stand for three kinds of knowledge. The first is sensible. The eye sees from afar what is outside it. The second is rational and is a great deal higher. The third corresponds to an exalted power of the soul, a power so high and noble it is able to see God face to face in his own self. This power has naught in common with naught, it knows no yesterday or day before, no morrow or day after (for in eternity there is no yesterday or morrow): therein it is the present now. (p.228)

St Augustine speaks of three kinds of knowledge. The first is corporal, form-seizing, like [that of the] eye which sees and receives images. The second is mental, but still aware of forms of corporal things. The third knowledge is interior, as it is in the spirit, that knows without form or likeness, and that knowledge is like unto the angels the host whereof is divided into three. (p.183 Book 2)

The Will

When is the will a saving will? The will is good and saving when it is impersonal, when, dead to self, it has been formed, transformed, into the will of God. (p.13 Book 2)

Will is to be taken in two senses. On the one hand, we have contingent will, non-essential will; on the other hand providential will, creative will, habitual will. It is not enough, in seeking union with God, to enjoy occasional detachment of mind, it needs expert, habitual detachment, going on before and after; then we receive great things from God and God in these things. To be unprepared is to lose the gift and God in the gift. This is why God cannot always give us things as we ask for them. It is no fault of his; he is a thousand times more ready to bestow than we are to receive. But we do him violence and wrong, hindering his natural work by our unreadiness. A man must learn in every gift to sacrifice himself to him, keeping nothing of his own and seeking nothing for himself, not profit nor enjoyment, nor inwardness nor sweetness nor reward nor heaven nor own-will. God never gave himself nor ever does in any other's will. He only gives Himself in his own will. Where God finds his will there he bestows himself, he lets himself in with all he is. And the more we die to our own the more do we really live in his. (pp.32-3 Book 2)

Commenting on St Peter's words, "See Lord, we have left all", when he had left merely his boat and net, a holy man (Hieronymus) observes: he who resigns the little of his own free will resigns not that alone: he is resigning all that worldly folk are out to gain, all they could possibly desire. But he who gives up his own will and himself to boot is giving up all things as surely as though they were his very own, his absolutely. (pp.5-6 Book 2)

Free Will

Why, man, what is the harm of letting God be God in you? Go clean out of yourself for God's sake and God will go clean out of his for your sake. Both being gone out, what remains is simply the one. In this one the Father gives birth to his Son, in his innermost source. Thence blossoms forth the Holy Ghost and thence originates in God the will belonging to the soul. The while this will remains unmoved by creatures and by creaturehood, the will is free. Christ says, "None goes to heaven but he who came from heaven." Things are all made from nothing; hence their true source is nothing. This noble will, as far as it inclines to creatures, with them elapses into nothing. (p.50)

Man has free will wherewith to make his choice between good and evil, and when God lays before him in ill-doing death and in well-doing life eternal, he must be free and master of his actions, no puppet dancing to another's piping. (p.35 Book 2)

Doctors declare this will is free in the sense that none can bind it saving God alone. God does not bind the will, he sets it free, free to choose naught but God himself, and this is real freedom. For the spirit to be incapable of willing aught other than God's will is not its bondage but its true liberation. Some people say, "If I have God and the love of God then I am at liberty to follow my own will." They labour under a mistake. So long as you are capable of anything against the will of God and against his law you have no love of God though you cozen the world that you have it. One who is in God's will and in God's love is fain to do the things God likes, and leave undone the things God hates, and he can no more leave undone a thing that God wants done than he can do a thing God abhors. Just like a man whose legs are tied together, he cannot stray and neither can he err who is in the will of God. (p.180)

The Strength of the Will

Where I cannot master God and bend him to my will it is because I fail either in will or meekness. I say, and I would stake my life upon it, that by will a man might pierce a wall of steel, and accordingly we read about St Peter that on catching sight of Jesus he walked upon the water in his eagerness to meet him. (p.133)

Will as will is not receptive, not in any wise: will consists in aspiration. (p.199)

Intellect

There is one power in the soul: intellect, of prime importance to the soul for making her aware of, for detecting, God. It has five properties. First, it is detached from here and now. Next, it is like nothing. Thirdly, it is pure and uncompounded. Fourthly, it is in itself active or self searching. Fifthly, it is an image. (p.114)

The soul knows no opposition when she enters the light of intellect. (p.207)

The Searching Intellect

Intellect peers in, it searches every corner of the Godhead

and finding the Son in the heart of the Father, in his ground, it takes him and sets him in its own. Intellect presses in; she is not content with good or wisdom, nor with truth nor yet with God himself. She is no more content with God than with a tree, a stone. She never rests until she gets into the ground whence truth and good proceed and takes them *in principio*, in the beginning, the fount of truth and goodness, where they rise before their coming forth: a ground far higher than truth and goodness are. Her sister (will) contents herself with God as being good. But intellect, leaving this behind, goes in and breaks through to the root whence shoots the Son and whence the Holy Spirit blossoms forth. (p.116)

Love turns to the loved: she finds there what is good. Intellect seizes the cause of good. Honey is sweeter in itself than anything we can make from it. Love takes God as being sweet; but intellect goes deeper and conceives him as being. (p.83)

The Resting Intellect

Above thought comes the intellect, as seeker. She goes about looking, casting her net here and there, gaining and losing. Above intellect the seeker there is another intellect which does not seek but rests in its pure and simple essence in the realm of light. (p.60)

A heathen philosopher observes: Intellect draws this veil [of goodness] from God and takes him bare, stripped of goodness, of being, and of every name. (p.212)

Intellect's object and sustenance is essence, not accident, just pure unadulterated being in itself. On descrying something real the intellect forthwith relies upon it, comes to rest thereon, pronouncing its intellectual word concerning the object attained. As long as intellect fails to find the actual truth of things, does not touch bedrock in them, it

113

stays in a condition of quest and expectation, it never settles down to rest, but labours incessantly to trace things to their cause, that is, it is seeking and waiting. It spends perhaps a year or more in research on some natural fact, finding out what it is, only to work as long again stripping off what it is not. All this time it has nothing to go by, it makes no pronouncement at all in the absence of experimental knowledge of the ground of truth. Intellect never rests in this life. However much God shows himself in this life it is nothing to what he really is. Truth lies in the ground but veiled and concealed from the intellect. And meanwhile the mind has no support to rest on as something permanent. It gets no rest at all, but goes on expecting and preparing for something still to come but so far hidden. There is no knowing what God is. Something we do know, namely, what God is not. This the discerning soul rejects. Intellect, meantime, finding no satisfaction in any mortal thing, is waiting as matter awaits form. As matter is insatiable for form, so is intellect unsatisfied except with the essential, all-embracing truth. Only the truth will do, and this God keeps withdrawing from it step by step, purposing to arouse its zeal and lure it on to seek and grasp the actual causeless good that, not content with any mortal thing, she may clamour more and more for the highest good of all. (pp.17-18)

Active and Passive Intellect

We were speaking just now of the active intellect and the passive intellect. Active intellect abstracts the image of outward things, stripping them of matter and of accidents, begetting their mental prototypes therein. And the passive intellect made pregnant by the active in this way, knows and cherishes these things with the help of the active intellect. Passive intellect cannot keep on knowing things unless the active intellect keeps on enlightening it. Now observe. What the active intellect does for the natural man that and far more does God do for the solitary soul: he turns out active intellect and installing himself in its stead he himself assumes the duties of the active intellect. (pp.16-17)

Her powers' [the soul's] perfection lies in the sovran power of intellect. This never rests. It wants God not as Holy Ghost nor yet as Son, it flees the Son. It wants God not as God. And why? Because thus he has name; were there a thousand Gods yet would it penetrate them all in the desire to get to where he has no name at all: it wants a noble, better thing than God as having name. What would it, then? It does not know: it would have him Father. "Lord, show us the Father," Philip cries, "and we shall be content." It wants him as the quick of kindness; it wants him as the marrow dripping fatness; it wants him as the root, the main of goodness: thus he is simply Father. (p.43)

Potential Intellect

Prithee, Sir, what is the use of my intellect if it has to be inert and altogether idle? Is it my best plan to raise my mind to the unknowing knowing which obviously cannot be anything? For if I knew anything it would not be ignorance, nor should I be idle and destitute. Must I remain in total darkness?

Aye, surely! You can do no better than take up your abode in total darkness and ignorance.

Alas, Sir! Must everything go then, and is there no return?

No, truly! By rights there is no return.

But what is this darkness? What does it mean? What is its name?

It can only be called a potential receptivity, which, however, is not altogether wanting in nor indigent of (real) being: the merely potential conception wherein you will be perfected. Hence there is no return from it. If you return it is not because of any truth, it is either the senses, the world or the devil. And persisting in her turning back, you inevitably lapse into sin and are liable to back-slide so far as to have the eternal fall. Wherefore there is no turning back, only a pressing forward and following up this possibility to its fulfilment. It never rests until fulfilled with all being. As matter never rests until fulfilled with every possible form, so intellect never rests till it is filled to the full of its capacity. (p.21)

Intellect in its potential power is like the angel's natural light, i.e. the evening light. With her actual power she raises all things up into God, where all things are bathed in the morning light. (p.86)

Man possesses an active intellect, a passive intellect and a potential intellect. Active intellect is ever in act, ever doing something, be it in God or in creature, to the honour and glory of God. That is its province and hence its name *active*. But when God undertakes the work the mind must preserve a state of passivity. Potential intellect again has regard to both these, to the action of God and the passion of the soul, to its acting potentially. In the one case the mind is active, when it is functioning, to wit; in the other receptive, when God takes up the work and then the mind ought, nay must, remain still and allow God to act. Now, before this is begun by the mind and finished by God, the spirit has prevision of it, potential knowledge of its happening. This is the meaning of potential intellect, which, however, is often neglected and does not bear fruit. When the mind is exerting itself in real earnest, God interests himself in the mind and its work, and then the soul sees and experiences God. But since the uninterrupted vision and passion of God is intolerable to the soul in this body, therefore God withdraws from the soul from time to time, as it is said, "A little while ye see me, and again a little while and ye do not see me". (pp.21-2 Book 1)

We recognize another power as being far removed from matter. How so? Suppose I saw a man twenty years ago, he may now be dead, but still I have a likeness of his form as though he stood before my eyes. This power needs no matter, but it has the imperfection of receiving from matter – in forms that is to say. On the other hand, the light, intelligence, transcends what is already matter or is so potentially. (p.105 Book 1)

Death of Intellect

Today we read in the gospel about the widow with an only son who had died. And our Lord came to him and said, "Young man, arise!" And he sat up.

By the widow we understand the soul; her husband was dead, so her son was dead also. Her son we take to mean her intellectual nature. Our Lord, sitting by the well, said to the woman, "Go home and fetch me thy husband". Not hers the living water which is the Holy Ghost; that is vouchsafed alone to those who are quickened in their understanding. Intellect is the summit of the soul. It has fellowship and intercourse with the angels in angelic nature. Angelic nature no time can touch, nor can time touch the intellectual nature. Unless she lives in this she will die. She was a widow. No creature lives but has some good and some shortcomings. She was a widow in this sense: intellect was dead in her, and with it perished also the fruit of it, the Son. (p.198)

Intellect higher than Will

I used to teach that intellect is higher than the will, both as belonging to this light. Another theologian . . . put will before the intellect on the ground that will enjoys things as they are in themselves, whereas intellect enjoys them as they are in it. That is quite true. The eye in itself is a better thing than the eye as painted on the wall. Nevertheless, I still maintain that intellect is higher than the will. Will takes God under the garment of good. Intellect seizes him naked, divested of good and being.

Theologians question whether the kernel of eternal life lies more in intellect or will. Will has two operations: desire and love. Intellect, with its simple function, is therefore better; its work is understanding, and it never stops until it gets a naked hold on what it sees. Withal it runs ahead of will and tells it what to love. We desire a thing while as yet we do not possess it. When we have it, we love it: desire then falling away. (p.117)

When the spark of the intellect carries right into God, then the man is alive (p.85)

Poverty

Two Kinds of Poverty

There are two kinds of poverty. One is outward poverty, and this is good and much to be commended in him who makes a voluntary practice of it for the sake of our Lord Jesus Christ whose wont it was on earth. . . . But there is another poverty, an interior poverty, where to refers this saying of our Lord "Blessed are the poor in spirit". (p.217)

Would you know what a really poor man is? Really poor in spirit is the man who prefers to do without all unnecessary things. Like the man who, sitting naked in his tub, said to mighty Alexander with the world beneath his feet, said he, "I am a greater man than you, for I have given up more than you have ever had. To me your proud possessions are beneath contempt." (p.39 Book 2)

Three Kinds of Poverty

A poor man is one who wills nothing, knows nothing, has nothing.

In the first place, a poor man wills nothing. Some folks mistake the sense of this; those, for example, who win personal repute by penances and outward disciplines. To all outward appearances these are holy, but they are fools within and ignorant of the divine reality. These people define a poor man to be one who wills nothing, explaining this to mean that he never follows his own will at all but is bent on carrying out the will of God. In this they are not bad; their intention is good and we commend them for it; God keep them in his mercy. But I trow these are not poor men nor are they the least like them. They are much admired by those who know no better, but I say they are fools with no understanding of God's truth. Peradventure heaven is theirs by good intention, but of the poverty in question they have no idea.

Suppose someone asked me, What then is a poor man who wills nothing? I should answer this. As long as it can be said of a man that it is in his will to do the will of God, that man has not the poverty I am speaking of, because he has a will, to satisfy the will of God, which is not as it should be. If he is genuinely poor, a man is as free from his created will as he was when he was not. I tell you by the eternal truth, as long as you possess the will to do the will of God and have the least desire for eternity and God, you are not really poor; the poor man wills nothing, knows nothing, wants nothing.

While I yet stood in my first cause I had no God and I was my own; I willed not, I wanted not, for I was conditionless being, the knower of my self in divine truth; then I wanted myself and wanted nothing else; what I willed I was and what I was I willed. I was free from God and all things. But when I escaped from my free will to take on my created nature, then I got me a God; for before creatures were, God was not God; he was that he was. When creatures became and started creaturehood God was not God in himself but he was God in creatures. Now we contend

119

that God as God is not the final goal of creatures nor such great riches as the least creature has in God. If a flea had intellect and could intellectually plumb the eternal abysm of God's being out of which it came, then, so we maintain, not God and all God is could fulfil and satisfy that flea. Wherefore we pray we may be quit of God and get the truth, and enjoy eternity, for the highest angel and the soul are all the same yonder where I was and willed that I was and was that I willed. Thus shall a man be poor of will, as little willing and desiring as he willed and wanted when he was not. And in this wise a man is poor who wills nothing.

Secondly, a poor man is one who knows nothing. We have sometimes laid it down that a man ought to live as though he lived not, whether for himself, or truth, or God. But now we change our ground and declare withal that a person in this poverty has got all he was when he lived not in any wise, not to himself, nor truth, nor God: he is so quit, so free of any kind of knowledge that no idea of God is alive in him; for while man stood in the eternal species God there lived none other in him: what lived there as himself. And so we say this man is as free from his own knowledge as he was when he was not; he lets God travail as he will while he himself stands idle as when he came from God. . . .

Thirdly, the poor man has nothing. It has often been said that perfection means not having the mortal things of earth, and haply this is true in one particular case, namely, when it is voluntary. But this is not the sense I mean it in. I have already said, the poor man is not he who wants to do the will of God but he who lives in such a way as to be free from his own will and from the will of God, even as he was when he was not. Of this poverty we say it is the deepest poverty. Secondly we say, that man is poor who has no knowledge of God's work in him. Being as free of knowing and perceiving as God is of all things is the barest poverty. But the third poverty, the straitest I am about to tell of, i.e. having nothing. (pp.218-20)

Here I would remind you how often I have said, and eminent authorities have said the same, that one must be devoid of things and of activities, both inwardly and outwardly, if one would be a fitting place for God to work in. Now we say something else. Granting a man is bare of everything, of creatures, of himself, of God, yet if it is still in him to provide God with the room to work in, then we do affirm: as long as this is in the man he is not poor with the strictest poverty. God does not purpose in his work that man should have in him the place God does his work in; poverty of spirit means freedom from God and all his works, so that if God chooses to travail in the soul he must be his own workshop, as he likes to be. Finding so poor a man, then God is his own patient and he is his own operating room, since God in himself is the operation. Here in this indigence man is obeying his eternal nature, that he has been and that he is now and that he shall be for ever. (p.220)

Five Kinds of Poverty

There are five kinds of poverty. The first is devilish poverty; the second is golden poverty; the third is willing poverty; the fourth is spiritual poverty; the fifth, divine poverty.

The first, or devilish, poverty, applies to all who have not what they fain would have, outward or inward. That is their hell.

The second, golden poverty, is theirs who in the midst of goods and properties pass empty out and in. If everything they own was burnt the effect on them would be to leave them quite unmoved. Heaven must needs be theirs and they would have no less.

The third is willing poverty and belongs to those who, renouncing goods and honours, body and soul, leave everything with right good grace. These give judgement with the twelve apostles and by pronouncing judgement it is their judgement day who, knowing what they leave, yet set another in their heart and mightily bestir themselves about their own departure. Such are the willing poor.

The fourth are spiritual poor. Those have forsaken friends and kindred, not merely goods and honour, body and soul; further, they are quit of all good works: the eternal Word does all their work while they are idle and exempt from all activity. And since in the eternal Word is neither bad nor good, therefore they are absolutely empty.

The fifth are godly-poor, for God can find no place in them to work in. Theirs is riddance without and within for they are bare and free from all contingent form. This is the man: in this man all men are one man and that man is Christ. (p.122)

6

The Soul

What is the Soul?

The soul is by nature heir to heaven. God is her lawful heritage, for no one generates the soul but God. (p.183)

The soul is created for good so great, so high that she cannot rest in any mode; all the time she is hastening past modes to the eternal good, to God who is her goal. (p.141 Book 1)

A heathen doctor says, If the soul knew herself she would know all things. (p.40)

The nature of the soul would never have gotten its kind were it not for her wanting to have God begotten in her; she would not have proceeded into her nature, would never have wanted to enter therein, except in the hope of this birth; nor would God ever have brought it to pass had he not meant the soul to be born into him. God does and the soul desires. God has the energy and the soul has the will and the power to have God born into her and herself into God. This God contrives with intent that the soul shall be like him. She needs must wait for God to be gotten in her and for her treasure to grow into God, desiring union and the safe-keeping of God. God's nature pours into the light of the soul and therein she is preserved. (p.65)

God is in the soul with his nature, his essence and his Godhood, but he is not on that account the soul. (p.143)

Plato says and with him St Augustine: The soul has all knowledge within and all we can do from without is but an awakening of knowledge. (p.104)

123

Beyond Time and Place

Soul is contained in a place as it were, between time and eternity, touching them both. With her higher powers she is in touch with eternity; in her inferior powers she is in contact with time. (p.73)

An ancient philosopher says the soul is made in between one and two. The one is eternity, ever alone and without variation. The two is time, changing and given to multiplication. He means to convey that the soul in her higher powers touches eternity, God to wit, while her lower powers being in contact with time make her subject to change and biased towards bodily things, which degrade her. Could the soul know God as well as the angels do she would never have come into the body. If she could know God without the world the world would not have been made for her sake. The world was contrived on her account for training and bracing the eye of the soul to endure divine light. (p.134)

The soul must put forth all her strength to lift herself above herself and be translated beyond time and place into the void where God is in and by himself, not going out nor eke in touch with any outside thing. (p.78)

I am as certain as I live, and as God lives, that the soul who knows him knows him above time and place. In this God-conscious state the soul perceives how near God's kingdom is, namely, God in all his fullness. There is much discussion among doctors at the School as to the possibility of the soul knowing God. Not by reason of his harshness does God exact so much from man but out of his great kindness, wanting the soul to be more capacious, big enough to hold the largesse he is anxious to bestow. (p.173)

The soul is created for good so great, so high that she cannot rest in any mode; all the time she is hastening past modes to the eternal good, to God who is her goal. (p.141)

Body and Soul

Because of the intimate union of the body and the soul the soul is in the smallest member as much as in the body as a whole. (p.73)

Body and soul are like twins, they being one man and born together, just as the other pair, Jacob and Esau, were born both at once, and they are opposed to one another. Esau is the trifler, one who occupies himself with frivolous and perishable things. Jacob is the fighter, the victor. Bersabee [the land of] stands for the uncertainty of this present world. On account of these things Jacob fled his country and his brother. Similarly with the soul, she is from heaven and body from the earth, from father and mother namely, and they are opposed to one another. Body wars with soul and soul with body, and according to St Paul there is bound to be strife between the soul and body. The soul desires eternal, the body temporal, things. The soul then has to flee from sensual pleasures and all impermanent things because, as Basilius has it, "Perfection means caring nothing for things which are not God". He gives four examples. The first: not caring for mortal things; next, vain glory, caring no more for his own repute than for his neighbour's. The third refers to pleasures of the senses. By these three he is taught to reach the fourth: caring nothing for himself. Thus the soul finds rest, and sleeping on a stone sees the ladder standing with one end on the earth and the other reaching up to heaven; sees the heavens open and God leaning over the ladder with the angels going up and down. (pp.210-11 Book 2)

Now turning to the soul, she has a drop of intellectual nature, a spark, a ray, and she has sundry powers which function in the body. One is the power of digestion, more active by night than in the day, whereby man grows and thrives. And the soul has a power in the eyes which makes the eye so sensitive and delicate and too fastidious to accept things in the coarse-grained mode they have themselves, but they must first be filtered and refined by light and air, owing to the presence in it of the soul. Another power in the soul is that wherewith she thinks. This power is able to picture in itself things which are not there, so that I can see the things as well as I see them with my eyes, or even better. I can see a rose in winter when there are no roses, therefore with this power the soul produces things from the non-existent, like God who creates things out of nothing! (p.212)

Penitential practices, among other things, were instituted for a special object. Fasting, watching, praying, kneeling, scourging, wearing of hair shirts, hard lying or whatever it may be, were all invented because body and flesh stand ever opposed to spirit. The body being far too strong for it, there is always battle joined between them, a never-ending conflict. Here the body is bold and strong for here it is at home; the world helps it, the earth is its fatherland, it is helped by all its kindred: food, drink, ease – all are opposed to spirit. The spirit is an alien here, in heaven are its kindred, its whole race; there dwell its loved ones. To succour the spirit in its distress and to impede the flesh somewhat in this strife lest it conquer the spirit, we put upon it the bridle of penitential practices to curb it, so that the spirit can control it. This is done to bring it to subjection; but to conquer and curb it and curb it a thousand times better, you put upon it the bridle of love. With love you overcome it most surely, with love you load it most heavily. God lies in wait for us therefore with nothing so much as with love. For love is like the fisherman's hook. To the fisherman falls no fish that is not caught on his hook. Once it takes the hook the fish is forfeit to the fisherman; in vain it twists hither and thither, the fisherman is certain of his catch. And so I say of love: he who is caught thereby has the strongest of all bonds and yet a pleasant burden. He who bears this sweet burden fares further, gets nearer therewith than by using any harshness possible to man. Moreover, he can cheerfully put up with whatever befalls, cheerfully suffer what God inflicts. Nothing makes you so much God nor God so much your own as this sweet bond. He who has found this way will seek no other. He who hangs on this hook is so fast caught that foot and hand, mouth, eyes and heart and all that is man's is bound to be God's. (pp.24-5)

Since God is love therefore he gives himself altogether. There is in the soul a natural likeness to this, for she exists in every limb and in each one whole. At her creation the soul is thus endowed in the ground of her being. So she can work in her members as a whole and in each one severally. (p.186 Book 2)

Spirit is a subtle thing, bringing life to all the limbs in virtue of the close accord of soul with body. (p.73)

Powers of the Soul

The highest power of the soul is the man, her will namely, which always stands bare and uncovered. The second power is intellect, the woman, who is always veiled, and the lower is raised up to the higher. Now when the power we call the man, i.e. the will, is joined to the power we call the woman, the intellect, that is to say, then the woman brings forth fruit in the perennial now. When the male is parted from the female power man's will is wavering in false light. (p.406)

There is a power in the soul untouched by time and flesh, flowing from the Spirit, remaining in the Spirit, altogether spiritual. In this power is God, ever verdant, flowering in all the joy and glory of his actual self. (p.36)

The soul has three powers: mind, will and rage. These three powers are in league with deity. Will cleaving unto God can do all things. God seized of his divinity bestows upon her power and fecundity. Mind cleaving to the Son knows with the Son; it knows with the Son when it is void of knowledge. The third power is the power of attack which is connected with the Holy Ghost. This power is ever making for the source whence it proceeded forth and the Holy Ghost is its initiator into the eternal nature; it floods the secret chamber of the soul, and lo! she loses time and place in the eternal, in time transcending time. (p.58)

The soul has three understandings. First, the understanding of things that are above her. Next, the understanding of herself. From this knowledge she passes to the third: the one alone. Therein she loses herself speaking never a word but possessing herself in silence, for God has rapt her up above herself to him; she is not and knows not by herself. (p.149)

St Augustine's explanation is as follows: Paul's being caught up into the third heaven merely refers to three kinds of knowledge belonging to the soul. The first is knowledge of creatures, which we can perceive with the five senses, and all things which are objective to mankind. Therein we see God but not all of him, only his dense body. The second knowledge is more spiritual, we have it of the absent, the consciousness, for instance, of a friend a thousand miles away of whom I have been thinking. I see him in imagination, his dress, his form, and in time and place. That too is nature. In this knowledge he is not intimately known, I cannot really know him by means of time or place or colour. The third heaven is purely spiritual knowledge, therein the soul is rapt away from all objective, bodily things. There we hear without means and see without matter; there there is no red or white or black or blue. In this pure perception the soul knows God altogether as one-fold in his nature and threefold in his Person. (p.207 Book 2)

The soul has something in her, a spark of intellect, that never dies; and in this spark, as at the apex of the mind, we place the paradigm of the soul; and there is also in our souls knowledge of externals, sensible and rational perception, present there as images and words which obscure it from us. (p.32)

The soul goes on beyond [the angels]. Suppose the soul to be identical with the highest human being here in time, nevertheless that man has the potential freedom to soar to untold heights above the angels, in the now of each, new without number, that is, without mode: above the angelic mode and every created intelligence. (p.30)

The soul is capable of knowing all things and she never rests till she attains her original form wherein all things are one; it is there she rests, in God. (p.75)

Aids and Hindrances to Union of the Soul with God

There are three hindrances to union of the soul with God. First her being too much divided, not simple (pure) enough. The soul is not simple in her relations with creatures. The second one is attachment to temporal things. And thirdly, being fond of the body will prevent union with God. Also there are in the soul three aids to union with God. First, the soul being one and undivided: to be atoned with God she has to be as pure as God is. Next, her being above herself and all temporal things and keeping hold of God. Thirdly, detachment from all mortal things and perfect freedom of action. (p.189 Book 2)

There are three reasons why my soul should hate herself. The first, that in so far as she is mine she is not God's. The second, because my soul is not wholly imbedded and set and re-cast into God. Augustine says, To have God for one's own one must needs first be God's. The third reason is the soul's enjoying herself as the soul while enjoying God with the soul, which is wrong. She should be enjoying God in herself since he is entirely hers. As Christ says, "He who loveth his soul shall lose it." What the soul is in this world or beholds in this world: things comprehended, apparent at all, she shall hate. A master declares that the soul at her

129

highest and purest transcends the whole world, nothing attaching the soul to the world but affection. Sometimes she has a natural love of the body. Sometimes she has a will inclined towards creatures. Another says the soul has no natural concern with the things of this world any more than the ear has with colour or the eye has with song. Our natural philosophers teach that the body is much rather in the soul than the soul in the body. Even as the cask contains the wine and not the wine the cask, so does the soul keep the body in her rather than the body the soul. What the soul loves in this world she is pure from by nature. According to one philosopher, it is the soul's nature and her natural end to achieve within herself a feat of understanding, God informing her with the general idea. He that can say he has attained his nature finds all things within himself, fashioned in light as they are in God; not as they are in nature but as they are in God. Neither spirit nor angel touches the ground or nature of the soul. In it she comes into the first, into the beginning, whence God breaks out in goodness into all her creatures. There she loves all things in God, not pure as they are in her uncompounded nature, but merely impartible as they are in God. (p.68)

St Augustine says, "Because the soul is greedy, because she wants to have and to hold so much, therefore she reaches into time and snatching at the things of time and number, loses what she already has." (p.227)

What She should Do

The soul must stop at home in her innermost, purest self; be ever within and not flying out: there God is present, God is nigh. (p.78)

The soul should dwell above herself and for four reasons. First for the manifold delights she finds in God. God's fullness is not able to contain itself, he must let creatures overflow from him, creatures to whom he can impart himself, who can receive his likeness, are poured forth without measure, enough, it would seem, to empty him: angels, more in number than seeds or leaves or grasses. Through them all light flows to us and gifts and grace. What flows through this nature God offers the soul and it would be as naught if he gave not himself in the gift.

Secondly, the soul ascends for the light she finds in God. All creatures are light in God. So sure as they flow out of God [they] are to God as naught to aught. In God is light and being, that is our darkness: naught, which in God is light, that is darkness.

Thirdly, the soul ascends for the *same* she finds in God, for there there is no *different*. Wisdom and goodness are the same in God. What wisdom is that very same is goodness and the rest. If in him wisdom were one thing and goodness were another there would be no satisfaction for the soul in God, but the soul has a natural inclination to God, and creatures all have an innate longing for wisdom. (p.187 Book 2)

She (the soul) takes four steps into God. At the first step she weakens in hope and desire and fear. At the next step hope, fear and desire vanish completely. The third step makes her all unmindful of them. The fourth step means oblivion, wherein she never thinks of them again. (p.188 Book 2)

The Spark of the Soul

The soul has a ghostly spot in her where she has all things matter-free just as the first cause harbours in itself all things immaterially. The soul also has a light in her with which she creates all things. When this light and this spot coincide so that each is the seat of the other, then, only then, one is in full possession of one's mind. (p.197)

According to the masters this light is of the nature of

unceasing effort; it is called "synderesis", that is to say a joining to and turning from. It has two works. One is remorse for imperfection. The other work consists in evermore invoking good and bringing it direct into the soul, even though she may be in hell. (p.88)

The soul, then, is the godly heaven and ghostly where in unbroken stillness God does his perfect work. As God spoke by the prophets, "Behold, I create in you a new heaven". (p.166 Book 1)

Godhead

Even so do all creatures speak God. And why do they not speak the Godhead? Everything in the Godhead is one, and of that there is nothing to be said God works, the Godhead does no work, there is nothing to do; in it is no activity. It never envisaged any work. God and Godhead are as different as active and inactive. On my return to God, where I am formless, my breaking through will be far nobler than my emanation. I alone take all creatures out of their sense into my mind and make them one in me. When I go back into the ground, into the depths, into the well-spring of the Godhead, no one will ask me where I came from or where I went. No one missed me. God passes away. (p.143)

What is the last end? It is the mystery of the darkness of the eternal Godhead which is unknown and never has been known and never shall be known. (p.224)

7

The Ending

The Godhead

The essence of the Godhead begets not. The Father's Person begets the Person of the Son eternally and together they pour forth their Holy Ghost. (p.148)

God and Godhead are as different as earth is from heaven. Moreover I declare: the outward and the inward man are as different, too, as earth and heaven. (p.142)

When God made man the innermost heart of the Godhead was put into man. (p.436)

While I subsisted in the ground, in the bottom, in the river and fount of the Godhead, no one asked me where I was going or what I was doing: there was no one to ask me. When I was flowing all creatures spoke God. If I am asked, Brother Eckhart, when did you go out of your house? Then I must have been in. Even so do all creatures speak God. And why do they not speak the Godhead? Everything in the Godhead is one, and of that there is nothing to be said. God works, the Godhead does no work, there is nothing to do; in it is no activity. It never envisaged any work. God and Godhead are as different as active and inactive. On my return to God, where I am formless my breaking through will be far nobler than my emanation. I alone take all creatures out of their sense into my mind and make them one in me. When I go back into the ground, into the depths, into the wellspring of the Godhead, no one will ask me whence I came or whither I went. No one missed me: God passes away.

All happiness to those who have listened to this sermon.

Had there been no one here I must have preached it to the poorbox. (p.143)

St Dionysius says, "The soul shall follow God into the desert of his Godhead, so far as here the body follows Christ in outward willing poverty." – "But that soul is idle." To which St Bernard answers: "Waiting upon God is not idleness but work which beats all other work to one unskilled in it." In order to find God we must seek him in his Godhead. Christ says, "If father or mother or anything else be a hindrance, quit them for good and serve God unhindered." The philosopher says, "The soul which is moved by the power of the Prime Cause need seek no counsel from any human wisdom; he is obeying what transcends wisdom, for he is moved by the latent, primitive truth." (p.44)

So nigh soul flows to God that many are deceived; but what she is she is by grace, and where she is by another's power. Yet she approaches near enough to God to be, in the power of the Father, invested with divinity by grace the same as the Father is by nature. St Paul says: "In the same image we shall go from one glory to another", meaning we shall receive divinity in its perfection and all that is consequent thereon. Therein she shall conceive divinity as it conceives itself and her will and God's will shall be one: whatever God may be we shall be with God. No one can attain it in this body, but when God gives the soul his final gift, the vision of his Godhead, the soul is raised up to the Trinity. (p.41)

Plato says, "the soul of all creatures is the Godhead". Then our Lord Jesus Christ is the soul of the elect. (p.450)

God dwells in the nothing-at-all that was prior to nothing, in the hidden Godhead of pure gnosis whereof no man durst speak. (p.41)

What is the last end? It is the mystery of the darkness of the eternal Godhad which is unknown and never has been known and never shall be known. Therein God abides to himself unknown, and the light of the eternal Father has been shining there for aye, and the darkness does not comprehend the light. May we find this truth, so help us, the truth whereof we speak. (p.224)

The Trinity

The Father's person begets the person of the Son eternally and together they pour out their Holy Ghost. (p.148)

The Father goes on begetting his Son in himself without ceasing, and Father and Son breathe forth with equal power their holy Breath, both Son and Holy Ghost abiding with the Father in the essence, and in the vision of this Trinity of Persons lies the whole happiness of creatures which are able to participate in his divine felicity. (p.170)

Deity flowed into the Father and into the Son and into the Holy Ghost: in eternity into itself and in time into creatures, to each as much as it can hold: to the stone its being, to the tree its growth, to beasts sensation, to the angels reason and to mankind all these four natures. (p.40)

From him applies to the Father, the origin of all things in eternity and in time. *Through him* applies to the Son through whom all things proceeded forth. *In him* applies to the Holy Ghost in whom all things are contained, made spirit and brought back to their end. (p.138)

The Sanctified City

He went to a city. I say that means the soul which is well ordered and fortified in the Holy Ghost and, having set a watch for sin and shut out multiplicity, is safe and sound in Jesus: encompassed and walled round by the light of God. (p.98)

Essence is self-absorbed, not an effusion but an inner fusion. And unity is one and self-contained: aloof from

every thing and free from outside intercourse. But goodness is the melting and running out of God; his diffusion to
the whole of creatures. Essence is the Father, unity the Son,
and goodness is the Holy Ghost. The Holy Ghost seizes the
soul (the sanctified city) at its purest, at its highest and
hales it up into its first source, which is the Son, and the
Son bears it on into his source, his Father namely, into the
ground, into the first, where the Son has his being; where
the eternal wisdom is in like repose in the holy and in the
sanctified city, in the innermost. (p.99)

God's being is fontal: flowing and fixed, final as well as
the first. From being power flows out into work. In this
sense the three Persons are the storehouse of divinity and
the three Persons are poured forth into the essence of the
soul as grace. God's being in the essence of the soul is the
imitation of the Persons and one being permeates the other.
Her chief power flows from the essence of the soul just as
the three Persons issue from the Godhead. (p.40)

According to the saints, power is in the Father, likeness
in the Son and union in the Holy Ghost. Hence, if the
Father is all present to the Son and the Son is all-to like
him, therefore no one knows the Father but the Son. (p.75)

The Real Truth

Now mark the signs whereby a soul is known to have been
taken into the Holy Trinity. First, it is vouchsafed to her
that at the sight of the Holy Ghost her sins are blotted out
and she forgets herself and things. In the next place she has
gotten a conception of the Godhead, namely the eternal
wisdom of the Father, the knowledge and discernment of
all things and she is bereft of opinion, hypothesis, belief,
for now she knows the truth; and whereas hitherto she has
taken things on trust and learnt by wordy arguments and
hearsay, now things presented to her, whether by men or
by angels, she need ask none about, like those with no

notion of reality, who, when an abstract truth is revealed to them, will try to grasp it with their finite mind, a thing that is beyond angelic understanding. (p.189)

I say concerning God's freedom that it yields no nature save one. God starts with the Son and the Son is another than the Father who is power, and from them twain there blossoms forth the Holy Ghost. Our philosophers teach that the sun draws the flowers out of the roots through the stem, timelessly well nigh and too subtly for any eye to follow. The soul, which has no nature in her ground, the ground of love, where she is love, emerges from this nature where she is stored in God. Whatever enters this being has much the same being. At the coming of the bride he devotes himself to her and works with all his might within his ground, in his innermost, where naught exists, where activity stops altogether. The tree of the Godhead grows in this ground and the Holy Ghost sprouts from its root. The flower that blossoms, love, is the Holy Ghost. In this Holy Ghost the soul flowers with the Father and the Son, and on this flower there rests and reposes the spirit of the Lord. He could not repose had he not rested first upon the Spirit. The Father and the Son rest on the Spirit, and the Spirit reposes upon them as its cause. (p.154)

Now we proceed to speak of the things of God, of Persons and of essence, which we hardly understand. Those that cannot follow this discourse can take refuge in the dogma I have taught before, that the three Persons are in one essence and one essence in the three Persons. Remember we are speaking of Father and paternity, and you must understand that these two are not apart in two hypostases, but they are one hypostasis, and moreover they are one and three rationally speaking. Consider the meaning of paternity. It means the power of father-kind. A father is known by the fact that he begets, but we recognize paternity in a potential father. Take, for example, the maid who is a virgin. By nature she is maternal though not

actually mother. The same thing with a father: in his power
to beget he is paternal, but the fact of his begetting makes
him father. Mark this difference between father and
paternity when the Word is gotten ghostly in the soul. This
we take to be the case when the soul, sublimed and in the
proper state, grows pregnant with God's light and divine
by nature: by the unique power of God grown big with
Deity. You see, in this immanent power, soul too is
paternal. But radiant with revelation, she with the Father
begets and is then with the Father called father.

This father and fatherhood differ as applied to the soul.
Mark, too, that Son differs from filiation, remembering
that these two are not separate in two hypostases: they are
the same hypostasis. We find filiation in potential father-
nature, unborn. If he were not unborn in his potential
nature the Father could not beget him, for a thing that
comes out must first have been in. So much for filiation.
But the Son we explain as the Father's begetting of his own
Word, whereby the Father is Father. The Son, moreover, is
God in himself, not God of himself but of the Father alone.
Were he God of himself he would not be one with the Father
so there would be two without any beginning. Which is impossible. We postulate three distinct properties, the Father's
property is that he comes from none but himself. The Son's
property is that he does not come from himself: he descends
from the father by way of nativity. The Holy Ghost's property is that he comes from the Father not as being born: he
proceeds from them twain, both Father and Son, not as a
birth but as love. For two who are sundered in Person
cannot together bear one but they can bear mutual love.
(pp.138-9)

The Circle

The bride says in the Book of Love, "I have run round the
circle and have found no end to it, so I cast myself into the
centre".

This circle which the loving soul ran around is all the Trinity has ever wrought.

Why is the work of the Trinity called a circle? Because the three Persons have wrought their own likeness in all creatures which are rational. The Trinity is the origin of all things and all things return into their origin. This is the circle the soul runs. When does she run in this circle? She does so when she muses: all this that he has made he could make again a thousand times if he were so minded. So she goes round in an endless chain. The least of all his creatures, she can find no end to nor can she approfound its worth. Spent with her quest she casts herself into the centre. This point is the power of the Trinity wherein unmoved it is doing all its work. Therein the soul becomes omnipotent.

The three Persons are one omnipotence. This is the motionless point and the unity of the Trinity. The circumference is the incompehensible work of the three Persons. The point is fixed. The union of the Persons is the essence of the point. In this point God runs through change without other-

ness, involving into unity of essence, and the soul as one with this fixed point is capable of all things. But her powers, wherein she imitates the Trinity, with them she cannot apprehend its unity. The work of the Trinity has proved the undoing of many Paris theologians: engrossed in the working of the Trinity they have never gotten at their unity. The centre is equally near to all ends, like time in all lands. *Now* is the time here and *now* is the same time in Rome. (p.357)

Death

Holy Death

The Kingdom of God is for none but the thoroughly dead. (p.419)

When, Lord, I was in you I was unnecessitous in my nothingness; it was your look, your notice of me, that made me indigent. If it is death for the soul to part from God, then it is death to her to emanate from God. All change is a dying. Wherefore we die from time to time and the soul dies all-dying in the wonder of the Godhead, impotently grasping at the divine nature. In the naught she is undone and comes to nothing. In this not-being she is buried, in un-knowing she is merged in the unknown, in unthinking merged in the unthought-of, in un-love one with the un-loved. Death's grip none can unloose: it severs life from limb and the soul from God and casts her into the Godhead wherein, sepultured, she is ignored by every creature. She is forgotten as one changed within the tomb nor is she held in any man's embrace. She like God is incomprehensible. For the dead who have died in the Godhead are beyond our ken, like the dead who die here to the body. That death is the soul's eternal quest. Slain in the three Persons she loses her naught and is hurled into the Godhead. (pp.384-5)

In Dying to Yourself you see God

What must a man be to see God? He must be dead. "No man can see me and live", said our Lord. Now St Gregory says, "That man is dead who is dead to the world". You can judge for yourselves how dead one may be and how little can touch us the things of this world. By dying to this world we do not die to God. (p.82 Book 1)

The soul must die if she is to grow receptive to another nature. You must be as the dead towards all happenings. God will never otherwise be your entire being. He may give you various gifts and light and comfort, much prized and very valuable things, but God will never give himself to you without reserve till you give yourself up altogether. As the soul dies in herself God comes to be her whole life, and

141

there will remain no more than one, as my body and my soul are no more than one. "He that hateth his soul shall keep it," says our Lord. (p.185 Book 2)

St Paul affirms of the holy martyrs and friends of our Lord, "They are dead." From this we argue that we have to be dead too. I hold that anyone who is not really dead has not the faintest notion of the sacred things revealed by God to his beloved. As long as you still know who your father and mother have been in time, you are not dead with the real death. Further I hold: as long as it affects you that no one will shrive you nor give you God's body nor shelter you from the world's scorn, as long as it is in you to be moved by this, know that you are a stranger to the true death. When you are aware of nothing within you: when having escaped from earthly species and forgotten your honourable estate and all temporal happenings, you have entered oblivion so deep that nothing formulates itself in you and you are sensible of nothing save the sheer ascension of your soul, then you can say that you are really dead. He who is dead thus is always the same; nothing affects him. About this St John says, "Blessed are the dead that die in God." See then, my friends, how good it is to die in God. We can die gladly if God will live and work in us while we are idle. We die, it is true, but it is a gentle death. (p.323)

As St Paul says, "God dwells in the light that no man can approach unto", which is in itself the perfect one. A man, then, must be dead, must be dead indeed, devoid of any being of his own, wholly without likeness, like to none, to be really Godlike. (p.182)

It behoves us to emulate the dead in dispassion towards good and ill and pain of every kind. (p.205)

Where two grow one, one loses its nature. Ergo, for God and the soul to be one, the soul has to lose her own life and nature. (p.27)

To subsist immediately in this pure nature a man must be so wholly dead to person that he wills as well to one across the seas whom his eyes have never seen as to his own present and familiar friend. (p.48)

There is no greater valour nor no sterner fight than that for self effacement, self-oblivion. (p.422)

Bodily Death

He [GOD] never destroys without providing something better. The martyrs died: they lost their life and found their being. (p.206)

Knowledge of creatures in God is the dawn. And when she knows God in himself as pure essence, that is high noon. It should be the soul's desire to see, as though in non-sense, this most noble being. We advocate dying in God to the end that he may raise us up to being which is better than life: the being our life subsists in, wherein our life is quickened into actuality. We ought to face death willingly and die in order to obtain a better resurrection. (p.206)

Eternal Life

St Paul says: I am sure that neither death nor affliction can separate me from what I have within me. (p.8)

Why I pray God to rid me of God is because condition-less being is above God and above distinction: It was therein I was myself, therein I willed myself and knew myself to make this man and in this sense I am my own cause, both of my nature which is eternal and of my nature which is temporal. For this am I born, and as to my birth which is eternal I can never die. In my eternal mode of birth I have always been, am now and shall eternally remain. That which I am in time shall die and come to naught, for it is of the day and passes with the day. (p.220)

Detachment

What then, I ask, is the object of absolute detachment? and I answer that the object of absolute detachment is neither this nor that. It is absolutely nothing, for it is the culminating point where God can do precisely as he will. (p.345)

Unchangeableness and complete detachment from creatures, that sets me nearest to God and to the summit of perfection. (p.143 Book 2)

The Way of Detachment

Detachment has four steps. The first breaks in and makes away with all man's perishable things. The second one deprives him of them altogether. The third not only takes them but makes them all forgotten as though they had not been, and all about them. The fourth degree is right in God and is God himself. When we get to this stage the king is desirous of our beauty. (p.217)

There is none happier than he who stands in uttermost detachment. No temporal carnal pleasure but brings some ghostly mischief in its train, for the flesh lusts after things that run counter to the spirit, and spirit lusts for things that are repugnant to the flesh. He who sows the tares of love in flesh reaps death, but he who sows good love-seed in the spirit reaps of the spirit eternal life. The more man flees from creatures the faster hastens to him their creator. Consider, all you thoughtful souls! If even the love which it is given to me to feel for the bodily form of Christ can keep us from receiving the Holy Ghost then how much more must we be kept from getting God by inordinate love of creature comforts. Detachment is the best of all, for it cleanses the soul, clarifies the mind, kindles the heart and wakes the spirit; it quickens desire and enhances virtue giving intuition of God; it detaches creature and makes her one with God; for love disjoined from God is as water in the fire, but love in union is like the honeycomb in honey. (p.347)

Keep yourself detached from all mankind; keep yourself devoid of all incoming images; emancipate yourself from everything which entails addition, attachment, or encumbrance and address your mind at all times to a saving contemplation wherein you bear God fixed within your heart as the object from which its eyes never waver; any other discipline, fasts, vigils, prayers or whatever it may be, subordinate to this as to its end, using thereof no more than shall answer for this purpose, so shall you win the goal of all perfections. (p.348)

I have read many writings of heathen philosophers and sages of the old covenant and the new and have sought earnestly and with all diligence which is the best and highest virtue whereby a man may knit himself most narrowly to God and wherein he is most like to his exemplar, as he was in God, wherein there was no difference between himself and God, before God created creature. And having approfounded all these scriptures to the best of my ability, I find it is none other than absolute detachment from all creatures. As our Lord said to Martha, "*unum est necessarium*", which is as good as saying, he who would be serene and pure needs but one thing, detachment. (pp.340-1)

I extol detachment above any love. First, because at best love constrains me to love God. Now it is far better my constraining God to me than for me to be constrained to God. My eternal happiness depends on God and me becoming one; but God is apter to adapt himself to me and can easier communicate with me than I can communicate with God. Detachment forces God to come to me and this is shown as follows. Everything is fain to be in its own natural state. But God's own natural state is unity and purity and these come from detachment. Hence God is bound to give himself to a heart detached – Secondly, I rank detachment above love because love constrains me to suffer all things for God's sake; detachment constrains me to admit nothing but God. Now it is far better to admit nothing but God than to suffer all things for God's sake. For in suffering one has regard to creatures whence the suffering comes, but detachment is immune from creature. Further, that detachment admits of none but God I demonstrate in this way: anything received must be received in aught. But detachment is so nearly naught that there is nothing rare enough to stay in this detachment except God. He is so simple, so ethereal, that he can sojourn in the solitary heart. Detachment then admits of God alone. (p.341)

Humility the masters laud beyond most other virtues. I rank detachment before any meekness and for the following reasons. Meekness can be without detachment but complete detachment is impossible without humility. Perfect humility is a matter of self-naughting; but detachment so narrowly approximates to naught that no room remains for aught between zero and absolute detachment. Wherefore without humility is no complete detachment. Withal two virtues are always better than one. Another reason why I put detachment higher than humility is this: humility means abasing self before all creatures and in that same abasement one goes out of oneself to creatures. But detachment abides in itself. Now no one going out, however excellent, but staying in is better still. As the prophet has it, "*Omnis gloria filiae regis ab intus*", the king's daughter is all glorious within. Perfect detachment is without regard, without either lowliness or loftiness to creatures: it has no mind to be below nor yet to be above; it is minded to be master of itself, loving none and hating none, having neither likeness nor unlikeness, neither this nor that, to any creature; the only thing it fain would be is *same*. But to be either this or that it does not want at all. He who is this or that is aught; but detachment is altogether naught. It leaves things unmolested. (p.341)

True detachment means a mind so little moved by what

befalls, by joy and sorrow, honour and disgrace, as a broad mountain by a gentle breeze. Such motionless detachment makes a man superlatively Godlike. For that God is God is due to his motionless detachment, and it is from his detachment that he gets his purity and his simplicity and his immutability. If then a man is going to be like God, so far as any creature can resemble God, it will be by detachment. (p.343)

Prayer

What is prayer? It is the practice of pure being and glorying therein. (p.96)

Ways to Pray

There is no true and perfect will, till entering wholly into God's will, a man has no will of his own. The more this is the case with him, the more and more safely he is established in God. One Ave Maria said thus, with self-forgetfulness, is better than a thousand said without, better one step in this way than a journey over seas in any other. (p.16 Book 2)

Quoth our Lord, "The hour cometh and is now when true worshippers shall worship not only on the mountains and in the Temple but in spirit, in the place of God". The moral of which is that we ought to pray to God not only on the hill-tops and in churches, but we ought always to be praying, at all times and everywhere. St Paul says, "Rejoice evermore; in everything give thanks; pray without ceasing." Even so pray those whose every deed is done like-mindedly for the love of God; who, careless of their personal pleasure, bow themselves humbly before God and leave him alone to act. The prayer of the lips was enjoined by holy Christendom for the recalling of the soul from her outward senses wherein she dissipates herself in a multiplicity of perishable things. Being recollected thence into her highest power (i.e. knowledge and memory and will) she is turned to spirit, and when the spirit is joined to God in perfect unity of will, it is turned to God. Then, not till then, he is in true prayer, when he has reached the goal of his creation, for we were created solely to be God, and that is the reason why we were fashioned like him. Whoso does not attain to being one with God in spirit is not a really spiritual man. (p.187)

The question is, does the virtue of prayer increase with the outside practice of it? Meister Eckhart says that the external habit adds little or nothing to the value of prayer. Prayer is a good thing in itself. Now a thing that is good in virtue of its muchness is not good in virtue of itself. One groat has little value all alone, but if you had a thousand groats that would be a handsome property, solely by reason of the number. Groats have small value in themselves apart from number. And so it is with outward practices: number adds little to the good of prayer; one Ave coming freely from the heart has greater power and virtue than a thousand from the lips. And by the same token, no virtue dwells in number of good works; virtue is every whit as fine, as good, in one least act of virtue rightly done as in a thousand. Virtue is not enhanced by multiplying outward acts of virtue, for were it good from number it would not then be good in its own right. A thing good in itself is good in its oneness not in its multiplication. True virtue means virtuous works wrought virtuously. Who gives an alms in God's name but gives it grudgingly and not with cheerful heart, what though he do a virtuous deed, he does not do it virtuously. And so with prayer or any other virtue: done rightly it is virtue but not else. Take patience for example. External suffering does not make one patient: it merely tries one's patience, as fire will try a penny, whether it be of silver or of copper. The patient man is patient still though outward suffering ne'er befall. And prayer the same. The man of pure heart Godward turned who never does a stroke of outside work is nevertheless in good case, for hearts are not made pure by outward prayers: prayer rises pure from pure hearts. (p.428)

When I pray for aught my prayer goes for naught; when I pray for naught I pray as I ought. When I am one with that wherein are all things, past, present and to come, all the same distance and all just the same then they are all in God and all in me. There is no thought of Henry or Conrad. Praying for aught save God alone is idolatry and unrighteousness. ... When praying for someone, for Henry or Conrad, I pray at my weakest. When praying for no one I pray at my strongest, and when I want nothing and make no request I am praying at my best, for in God there is no Henry, no Conrad. To pray to God for aught save God is wrong and faithless, and, as it were, an imperfection. (p.27)

Never pray for any mortal thing; if you must pray for anything at all, pray for God's will and nothing else for therein you have all. To ask for anything besides means getting nothing. (p.140)

I vow I will not pray to God for gifts nor worship him because of gifts bestowed, but I will entreat him to make me worthy to receive, and worship him for being of the essence and of the nature that must give. (p.44)

Our theologians ask, what praises God? Likeness does. Any likeness to God that lives in the soul redounds to the glory of God. Things at all different from God do not glorify God. A portrait, for example, reflects credit on the painter who embodies it in his dearest conception of his art and makes it the image of himself. The likeness of the portrait praises the author without words. Of little worth is spoken praise or praying with the lips. Our Lord said on one occasion, "Ye pray, not knowing what prayer is. There shall come again true prayers, praying to my Father not in words but in spirit and in truth." What is prayer? Dionysius says, "The mind's ascent to God, that is what prayer means." It is a heathen who observes that where spirit is and unity and eternity there God will be at work. Where flesh is warring against spirit; where disruption is warring against union; where time is warring with eternity, there God works not. He can do nothing with it. (p.97)

Body and Prayer

The most powerful prayer, one well-nigh omnipotent, and the worthiest work of all is the outcome of a quiet mind. The quieter it is the more powerful, the worthier, the deeper, the more telling and the more perfect the prayer is. To the quiet mind all things are possible. What is a quiet mind? A quiet mind is one which nothing weighs on, nothing worries, which, free from ties and all self-seeking, is wholly merged into the will of God and dead as to its own. Such an one can do no deed however small but it is clothed with something of God's power and authority. It behoves us to pray hard so that all our mortal members with their powers – eyes, ears, heart, mouth, and all their senses – are turned in that direction, and we must never stop until we find ourselves on the point of union with him we have in mind and are praying to, God namely. (p.4)

Thomas says that prayer simply means climbing up to God. God says that he is high and man is low; so for a man to get to God he must put something under him that will make him higher. He has to put under him the things that God has made, even the soul herself as to her powers, whose work can never be perfect in the body. I refer to sight and hearing and [the rest of] the five senses, which link up soul and body. The soul must withdraw into those powers which can function to perfection in the body, i.e. love and knowledge. In these twin powers the soul pours out of (and dies to) the world. For knowing God I want no

150

eyes (or ears): that needs another, spiritual, knowing. To be atoned with God in love I need no hands or feet nor any limbs whatever, but stealing forth of all created things man locks his spirit up alone with God. That is true prayer, and that alone, and only in that prayer will God be moved to listen to man's longings or answer his entreaties, for above (time) and place God does his godly work alone in me. (p.200 Book 2)

Contemplation

People often say to me: "Pray for me." And I think to myself: Why ever do you go out? Why not stay at home and mind your own treasure? For indeed the whole truth is native in you. (p.50)

In the contemplative state we are consumed by fiery love in the Holy Ghost. Sooner than knowingly commit a sin, venial or mortal, we shall prefer to suffer every imaginable martyrdom. If by one venial sin we were enabled to release from hell souls without number, we would not ransom them. Such love to God must a man have to be familiar with him in contemplation. Moreover, he must have a mind at ease; and in preparing for it, an undisturbed retired spot is necessary. The body should be rested from bodily labour, not only of the hands but of the tongue as well and all five senses. The soul keeps clear best in the quiet, but in jaded body is often overpowered by inertia. (p.46)

*

According to Meister Eckhart there are seven degrees of contemplation.

Whoso would practise contemplation let him seek out a quiet spot and set himself to thinking, first, how noble his soul is, how she has flowed straight out of God, a thought that fills him with a great delight. Having well cogitated this, next let him think how God must love his soul to make it in the likeness of the Trinity, so that all God is by nature he may be by grace; whereat he will delight perforce more vehemently still for it is far more noble to be made in the form of the Trinity than merely to come straight from God. In the third stage he meditates that he has been beloved of God for aye; the Trinity has been for aye and God has loved his soul for aye. Fourthly, he reflects that God did ever charge him to enjoy with God what God has aye enjoyed and always shall, God himself namely. At the fifth stage the soul enters into herself and knows God in herself, which happens in this wise: No being can be without being and being feeds on being; but being cannot live upon this food till this food is converted to the same blessed nature as that which feeds upon it and this applies to being which is being-of-itself. But there is no being-of-itself excepting God. So my soul is living on nothing but God. And by entering into oneself like this one finds God in oneself. If God will that I faint not he must give me being. No being can stand without God so if he means me to have being he must give me himself.

The sixth stage is, soul knows herself in God. As thus. Everything in God is God. Now my idea has always been in God, is still and ever shall be, therefore my soul is ever one with God and is God and I do find myself in God in the exalted fashion of being God in God eternally. This brings the expert soul ineffable delight.

At the seventh stage the soul knows God in himself as being without beginning whence all things emanated. This gnosis comes to no man fully in this life for it means the beholding of God, a thing not of this world. (pp.433-4)

While we are in sight of, we are not one with, what we see. While we notice anything we are not one with it. Where there is no more than one, no more than one is seen: God is not seen except by blindness, not known except by ignorance, not understood except by fools. (p.188)

David says that man rising to the summit of his mind is exalted God. From this divine eminence we see the lowness and insignificance of creatures. We feel an inkling of the perfection and stability of eternity, for there is neither time nor space, neither before nor after but everything present in one new, fresh-springing *now* where millenniums last no more than the twinkling of an eye. (p.47)

So we fall into peculiar wonder. In this wonder let us remain, for human wit is powerless to fathom it. Plumbing the deeps of divine wonder but stirs facile doubt. (p.47)

Common Sense

No person can in this life reach the point at which he is excused from outside works. What though one lead the contemplative life, one cannot altogether keep from flowing out and mingling in the life of action. Even as a man without a groat may still be generous in the will to give, whereas a man of means in giving nothing cannot be called generous, so no one can have virtues without exercising virtue at the proper time and place. Hence those who lead the contemplative life and do no outward works are most mistaken and all on the wrong tack. What I say is that he who lives the contemplative life may, nay he must, be absolutely free from outward works what time he is in act of contemplation but afterwards his duty lies in doing outward works; for none can live the contemplative life without a break, and active life bridges the gaps in the life of contemplation. (p.425)

When a man delights to read or hear tell about God, that comes of divine grace and is lordly entertainment for the soul. To entertain God in one's thoughts is sweeter than honey, but to be sensible of God is teeming consolation to the noble soul, and union with God in love is everlasting joy which we relish here as we are fitted for it.

They are all too few who are fully ripe for gazing in God's magic mirror. Precious few succeed in living the contemplative life at all here on earth. Many begin but fail to consummate it. Because they have not rightly lived the life of Martha. As the eagle spurns its young that cannot gaze at the sun, even so fares it with the spiritual child. (p.44)

Maybe you will say, I gather then that prayers and virtuous deeds are all in vain; God takes too little interest in them to be affected by them. And yet they say God likes to be entreated on all occasions.

Now mark, and realize if possible, that in his first eternal glance (if a first glance may be assumed), God saw all things as they would happen and he saw in that same glance both when and how he would make creatures. He saw the humblest prayer that would be offered, the least good deed that anyone would do and saw withal which prayers and which devotions he would hear. He saw that tomorrow you will call upon him earnestly, urgently entreating him, and not for the first time tomorrow God will grant your supplication and your prayer: he has granted it already in his eternity before ever you became man. Suppose your prayer is foolish and lacking in earnestness, God will not deny it you then, he has denied it you already in his eternity. (pp.343-4)

Grace

One master says: Grace is the face of God which is clearly stamped on the soul without any means by the Spirit of God, giving the soul the form of God. (p.56)

Grace comes from God

By grace man may be carried to the length of understanding as St Paul understood, who was caught up into the third heaven and saw unspeakable things. (p.54)

One master says: Grace springs from the heart of the Father and flows into his Son and in the oneness of those two it proceeds from the Wisdom of the Son into the gift of the Holy Ghost and in the Holy Ghost is sent into the soul. (p.56)

When the soul is dead in imperfection, the higher mind awakening into understanding cries to God for grace. (p.100)

So nigh flows the soul to God that many are deceived; but what she is she is by grace, and where she is she is by another's power. Yet she approaches near enough to God to be, in the power of the Father, invested with divinity by grace the same as the Father is by nature. (p.41)

Some things God does with help of creature and some unaided. If the grace which is a help and which is coming through my words could enter your heart without means, as though spoken by God, your soul would forthwith be converted and she could not help it. By pronouncing God's word I become a co-worker with God and grace is mingled in me, God speaking it through me, and since I am to you as the means, it is not received intact in your soul. But the grace which is uttered by the Holy Ghost itself is received direct and imprinted unaltered in the soul what time the soul is recollected into the single power which has intuition of God. (p.159)

According to St Augustine, "God hides in the recesses of the soul, disguised in the workings of grace wherein he shows himself to the soul covertly, so that none may know except the soul wherein he is thus privily concealed." (p.166)

Beyond Understanding

According to the philosopher who is our chief authority upon the soul, no human wisdom ever can attain to what the soul is. That requires supernatural wisdom. What the powers of the soul issue from into act, we do not know: about it haply we do know a little, but what the soul is in her ground no man knows. Any knowledge thereof that may be permitted to us must be supernatural; it must be by grace: God's agent of mercy. (p.177)

Beyond Intellect

There is another light, the light of grace, compared to which this natural light illumines a mere pin-point of the earth, nay rather a mere pin-point compared with the whole heavens which are incredibly more vast than all the earth. God's presence in the soul by grace is instinct with more light than any intellect can give: the light of intellect is but a drop in the ocean of this light, nay less a thousand-fold. Hence to the soul who is in God's grace all things, and whatever her mind can grasp, will appear small and mean. (p.178)

Grace enters neither into intellect nor will. For grace to enter into intellect and will intellect and will must transcend themselves. A master says, "There is I know not what, wholly mysterious, above them", meaning the spark of the soul, the only part of her which is God-receptive. Here in this minute spark, called the spirit of the soul, there occurs true union between the soul and God. Grace never did any virtuous work: it has never done any work at all albeit good works are the outcome of it. Grace does not unify by works. Grace is the inhabiting and co-habiting of the soul in God. Work of whatever kind, external or internal, is beneath it. (p.200)

The Man in a State of Grace is Detached

To the soul with God's grace all things are [pleasant] to leave because creature can cause her no pain. (p.179)

156

Take now the first words spoken by the angel, "Elizabeth shall bear a child." From Elizabeth we know the condition of the soul wherein God's grace is born. John means grace-containing. "The child shall be great, born full of grace." Three sorts of birth are pure from the mother's womb. St John was [born] so pure that he could do no mortal sin; our Lady too was full of grace, she never committed any sin at all, mortal or venial; and our lord Jesus Christ was absolutely pure, gotten as he was of one so purified for his conception that he was never subject to original sin. Just as the virgin was detached so that soul must be in whom God's grace is to be born, not occupied with pleasant and unpleasant thoughts of people but intent on God alone. (p.177 Book 2)

How to Recognize the Man in Grace

By three things we know there is grace in the soul. First, by her being like God, for she is descended from divinity. Secondly, by her behaving like God, God's likeness stamped in the soul making her so much like God that to the devils she is presented as God, so noble the nature of grace. Thirdly, by the fact that the soul is not content unless it has all perfection at once, for, as the heathen philosopher says, "Perfection of soul means having likeness to God's angel as well to all creatures". (p.178 Book 2)

The Function of Grace

Now let us see how grace operates in the soul. We may compare it with an axe. This requires three things: first it must be well trimmed and polished. And so must the soul be stripped clean of sins, not able to sin, for the man of sin cannot do right without grace, without divine likeness; however much good he may do it will profit him nothing. This axe, again, brings about the workman's desired end.

Even so grace brings the soul into God; it transports the soul over herself and robs her of self and of all that is creature, and unites her with God. Grace works with the soul till she herself has to make room, and nothing is left there but God and the soul. (p.178 Book 2)

God's ultimate purpose is birth. He is not content until he brings his Son to birth in us. Nor is the soul content until the Son of God is born in her. It is thence grace springs. Grace is infused therein, grace doing nothing: its work is its becoming. It flows out of the essence of God and into the essence of the soul, not into her powers. (p.227)

What though a man have all the world yet must he look upon himself as poor and all the time be reaching out his hand before the door of our Lord God, asking for the grace of God, soliciting his alms, for grace makes men God's children. . . . It is impossible for any soul to be free from sin without the protection of God's grace. The function of grace is to quicken the soul and fit her for all divine uses, for grace flows out in a divine stream which savours of God and is a likeness of God and makes the soul God-like. When grace with its savour is warped into the will it is called love, and when this grace with its savour is warped into the intellect it is called the light of faith, and this same grace and savour warped into the irascible power goes by the name of hope. These divine virtues are so called because they do divine work in the soul, just as we see with the light of the sun its energizing action on the earth, giving life to everything and keeping it in being. If this light goes, everything goes, as though it were not. And so with the soul. Where grace is and love things are easy to do. It is a sure sign if a man finds good works hard to do that there is no grace in him. (p.179 Book 2)

When the time was fully come grace was born. (p.227)

Transcending Grace

One must abound in light and grace before one can see God. Grace is a surpassing light, superangelic. In grace we can see God but from afar. (p.112)

Our Lord upbraided his apostles saying, "There is still in you but a little light". They were not devoid of light, but it was weak, the light of grace, the brightest thing God ever made or ever could have made. And after all the soul is small so long as she is still in grace. Sometime or other the soul must rise in grace. If grace is not yet overcome, the soul has still to ascend in grace and, being perfected, to transcend grace: then she sees God. (p.112)

Grace does not destroy nature, it consummates it. Glory does not destroy grace, it finishes it, for glory is perfected grace. (pp.35-6 Book 2)

Peace

It is good to pass from restlessness to calm; praiseworthy but imperfect. "Go in peace. Be not disquieted": God implies that we ought to enter into peace and continue in peace and end in peace. God said, "In me ye have peace". So far in God, so far in peace. Is aught in God, it is in peace; is aught out of God, it is without peace. St John says, "Whatever is born of God overcometh the world". What is born of God seeks peace and ensues it. He that pursues the even tenor of his way and is at peace is a heavenly man. Heaven constantly rotates, in its motion seeking rest. (p.175)

Once a thing is in God it has peace; so far in God so far in peace. Judge then from time to time how far you are in God or otherwise, where you have peace or not. Where you have unrest there you must be restless: unrest comes from creature not from God. There is nothing in God to be afraid of: everything in God is altogether lovable. Neither is there any cause for sorrow.

He who has all he will, his every wish, that man has peace. None has it but the man whose will and God's are wholly one. God grant us this at-one-ment. (pp.41-2 Book 2)

Lastly, creatures are all seeking rest whether they know it or not. Never is the stone bereft of motion while it is not lying on the ground. And similarly fire. All creatures also: they seek their natural place. The loving soul finds rest nowhere except in God. David says, "God has ordained to everything its place: to fish the water, birds the air and beasts the earth and to the soul the Godhead." And Job declares in the same strain, "What is in God he gives us for our joy and bliss". God grant us peace and rest in him. So help us the eternal truth, which is himself. Amen.